LANGUAGE REVITALIZATION AT TRIBAL COLLEGES
AND UNIVERSITIES: OVERVIEWS, PERSPECTIVES,
AND PROFILES, 1993-2018

Tribal College Press is an imprint of *Tribal College Journal of American Indian Higher Education*, the publication of the American Indian Higher Education Consortium. For more information visit tribalcollegepress.org.

TRIBAL COLLEGE PRESS

Rachael Marchbanks, publisher

Bradley Shreve, PhD, managing editor

Marvene Tom (Diné), office manager

ADVISORY BOARD

Sherry Allison, PhD (Diné)
President, Southwestern Indian Polytechnic Institute

Carrie L. Billy, JD (Diné)
President and CEO, American Indian Higher Education Consortium

Pearl Brower, PhD (Iñupiat)
President, Iḷisaġvik College
Tribal College Journal Advisory Board Chair

Elmer Guy, PhD (Diné)
President, Navajo Technical University

Cynthia Lindquist, PhD (Spirit Lake Dakota)
President, Cankdeska Cikana Community College

Richard Littlebear, EdD (Northern Cheyenne)
President, Chief Dull Knife College

Paul F. Trebian, EdD (Tlingit)
President, College of Menominee Nation

Laurel Vermillion, PhD (Standing Rock Sioux)
President, Sitting Bull College

On the Cover: *Them Guys, Discussin* by Sam English (Ojibwe)

LANGUAGE REVITALIZATION AT TRIBAL COLLEGES AND UNIVERSITIES
OVERVIEWS, PERSPECTIVES, AND PROFILES
1993-2018

Edited by Bradley Shreve

TCP TRIBAL COLLEGE PRESS | MANCOS, COLORADO

© 2019 by Tribal College Press

Tribal College Press
130 E. Montezuma
Mancos, CO 81328

www.tribalcollegepress.org

ISBN: 978-0-9845472-3-4

Published in the United States of America

CONTENTS

FOREWORD
    Richard Littlebear | ix

INTRODUCTION | xiii

OVERVIEWS | 1

New Voices, Ancient Words: Language Immersion Produces Fluent Speakers, Stronger Personal and Cultural Identities
    Janine Pease | 3

Native Languages and Tribally Controlled Colleges: Giving Voice to Native Nations
    Paul Boyer | 11

More than Words, A Way of Life: Language Restoration Programs Reach Beyond Tribal Colleges and Universities
    Laura Paskus | 38

VOICES | 47

Finding a Place for Navajo: English Must Be Restricted if the Navajo Language Is to Survive
    Clay Slate | 50

To Save Our Languages, We Must Change Our Teaching Methods
    Richard Littlebear | 61

Who Will Teach My Great-Great Grandchildren Dakotah?
    Tammy Eastman DeCoteau | 64

One Man, Two Languages: Confessions of a Freedom-Loving Bilingual
    Richard Littlebear | 66

"We Are Resilient, and We Are Succeeding": A Statement before the Senate Committee on Indian Affairs
    Thomas Shortbull | 70

"To Revitalize Our Languages, We Must Work at All Levels": A Statement before the U.S. Senate Committee on Indian Affairs
    Clarena M. Brockie | 78

Native Languages Preserve Our Way of Thinking and Knowing
    Richard B. Williams | 88

PROFILES | 91

Learning Lodge Institute: Montana Colleges Empower Cultures to Save Languages
    Paul Boyer | 94

Rekindling the Anishnabe Language Fires at Bay Mills
    Jennifer Dale | 101

Using Blackfoot Language to Rediscover Who We Are
    Duane Mistaken Chief Sr. | 105

Little Priest Immerses Students in Language | 109

Giving Voice to Crow Country: The Crow Place Name Project
    Carrie Moran McCleary | 111

Back from the Brink: Innovative Language Program Involves Three Generations
    Ron Selden | 117

Teasing Aside: Little Big Horn College Maintains Crow Language, Culture
    Luella Brien | 120

Language of the People Forever: Bay Mills Spins Thread Tying Ojibwa Communities Together
    Brenda Austin | 122

Firing Up White Clay: Immersion School Students Encouraged to Return, Give Back
    Kurt Umbhau | 127

Ojibwemotaadidaa: Preparing a New Generation of Fluent Speakers
    Persia Erdrich | 131

Louis Soop and Language Restoration at Red Crow Community College
    Mary Weasel Fat | 135

Blackfeet Community College Develops Montana's First Native Language App | 138

Iḷisaġvik College Offers Language Nest Program
    Devin P. Bates | 139

Lakota Documentaries: Working with Cultural Heritage at a Tribal University
    Jurgita Antoine | 141

A Rebirth for the Lakota Language: Institute Hopes to Create a New Generation of Speakers
    Christopher Vondracek | 146

RESEARCH | 151

Native American Language Immersion: Innovative Native Education for Children and Families
    Janine Pease | 153

FOREWORD

Haahe, va'óhtama netamáhehetatseme. He'tohe móxo'èstoo'e móxhoestomase, ve'éšehene'enováhehene. Xamaavo'èstaneo'o hapo'e
Ešeeveasètotoxèstanovóhtse tsehe'enóstsevóse. Hene ema'xèpèheva'e!

Greetings, I say "welcome" to all of you readers. When you read this book, learn from it. It was written by Indigenous people who are writing about their languages. Indigenous people writing about their own languages is a very good thing.

In the early 1980s, I could not have written what I wrote above. I did not know how to write my own language and there were no compilations of writings by our own Indigenous people writing about our own languages. I read articles about the acquisition of the Spanish language or some of the southeastern Asian languages, about German and French, but no narratives about the Cheyenne language or any other language native to the Americas. I'm sure they were there somewhere but, for the most part, they seemed not to exist at all.

I did try to read the Cheyenne language but found the writing system that was used incomprehensible. A linguistic writing system that was introduced in the 1970s was more comprehensible to me so I started learning how to write my own language. But let me back up a little bit.

Up until the late 1970s and early 1980s, I advocated teaching and learning only English. I'd been trained as an English grammar and literature teacher and those were the aspects of a language I advocated. When I looked around our village, I saw that those who spoke English had the better lifestyles, the better jobs, and were better educated. Thus I came to the conclusion that being able to use the English language could lead to a better life.

However, after a series of epiphanies I concluded that the educational systems, the mainstream culture, the religious institutions, and the job markets had been lying to us. I concluded that speaking my own language did not present a danger to me but that it represented a danger to other people, especially those from the mainstream society. I became an advocate of the Cheyenne language and, later, an advocate for all Indigenous languages and I am still an advocate.

So I am very encouraged by the articles in this book because they discuss in depth what our languages mean to us. The writers of these articles give us insights as to the best methods for perpetuating our languages and, thus, our cultures. They write about the issues that surround language teaching and they couple the teaching with our identities which have taken a severe battering by various language oppression policies. The authors write about identity, immersion, and teaching techniques within the immersion methods.

As Dr. Janine Pease writes in "New Voices, Ancient Words: Language Immersion Produces Fluent Speakers, Stronger Personal and Cultural Identities":

> It's quite important to understand what language immersion is not. It is not: lists of vocabulary words to memorize and phrases to translate; 40-minute classes five time a week; word searches in a two-way dictionary; digression into English to explain a word or phrase; drills in the structure of the language, like conjugation of verbs. Participants think and speak in the Native language, without translation time delays. The Native language is not a "subject" but the medium through which all subjects are instructed. Math, science, art, and music are taught in languages such as Blackfeet or Native Hawaiian. The Native language is the language of learning, interactions, and all communications.

The following anecdote about the immersion technique comes from an experience I had in Hawaii while touring one of the Punana Leo language teaching sites: A young boy was our guide. The fact that he was so knowledgeable about the site intrigued me so I asked him about his schooling. He said that he'd graduated and had been accepted at Stanford University. I thought that was quite an accomplishment but what he said next astonished me. He said he'd taken all of his courses in the Hawaiian language and all of his courses had been accepted by Stanford. It became clear to me the power of the immersion technique when it is applied correctly.

The other aspect of our languages that needs continuous reinforcement is the acquisition of a positive cultural and self-identity for each one of us. Whether we assimilate or not, it will be on our terms when it comes to issues that surround our languages. In "Native Languages and Tribally Controlled Colleges: Giving Voice to Native Nations," Paul Boyer illustrates this succinctly when he writes:

> By the late 1960s it was clear that Indians had not assimilated into mainstream society, despite centuries of effort by European colonists and the American government. They still existed as separate people and as a distinctive culture. But it was also clear that the unrelenting pursuit of assimilation had left a vast landscape of poverty, dependency, and social fragmentation. In this era of protest and social reform, a cadre of young tribal members rejected government control of Indian communities and offered a different strategy: they believed tribes should take charge of their own development and rebuild pride in their Native identities. The future depended upon building, not destroying, tribal nations and embracing, not rejecting, cultural traditions. The goal was not assimilation, but tribal self-determination.

The belief in taking charge of our own development and rebuilding pride in our Native identities is going to take a lot of work, especially when it comes to perpetuating our languages. The passage of time is our enemy now. A recent *National Geographic* article stated that at least one world language dies every two weeks. If there are 6,000 languages still extant, the article also stated that half of those will be gone by the end of this century. These are dire predictions, but we can save our languages if we just set our minds to thwart these predictions. Reading the following articles, heeding and acting on their content and recommendations, make this book a powerful resource. This resource will prevent us from joining the chorus of doomsayers who predict the inevitability of us losing our languages and our cultures.

About 20 years ago, whenever I would call a meeting to discuss the state of our Cheyenne language there would be about five people who would attend, and they were not always the same people at each meeting. Now we have a large group that attends regularly because they are concerned. I persisted for the past 20 years and I am gratified that the Northern Cheyenne people are realizing what we will lose if the Cheyenne language becomes extinct as an oral, conversational language.

I want our Cheyenne stories to be told in our language. I want the tribal council to hold their sessions in our language. I want the preachers to speak our language to their congregations. I want our rituals and our ceremonial rites to be spoken in our language. I want our teachers to teach their subject material in the Cheyenne language. I want all of these groups to read this wonderful compilation of grassroots-based articles that are contained in this book.

However, what would make me happiest would be to have a 6-year old child laugh uproariously at the right times when a funny story is told entirely in Cheyenne.

Richard Littlebear, EdD, is president of Chief Dull Knife College.

INTRODUCTION

Tribal colleges and universities (TCUs) collectively are doing more to revitalize North America's Indigenous languages than any other institutions. They are uniquely positioned for this great task—they are situated on tribal lands, have culturally rooted curricula, and are truly community colleges where tribal members and elders play a vital role in the classroom and in every day college life. Perhaps most importantly, tens of thousands of students are immersed in this inimitable environment every year, hearing, learning, and speaking Indigenous languages.

Since the founding of Navajo Community College 50 years ago, language revitalization and preservation has been an integral part of every tribal college's mission. It's one of the founding principles of the American Indian Higher Education Consortium, which today represents the nation's 37 TCUs and advocates on their behalf. In some communities, tribal colleges are the only institutions working to revitalize and preserve language, and to develop high-quality programs for their instruction. To be sure, it's a difficult task, but after a century of industrial school education, policies of assimilation, and concerted attempts to eradicate Indigenous languages, it's an essential one and vital for the well-being and vivification of Native Nations.

Many elders and academics alike agree that language is central to culture, that it serves as the binding force which gives a people self-awareness and a strong sense of identity. In his article, "Using Blackfoot Language to Rediscover Who We Are," Duane Mistaken Chief Sr., a longtime educator at Red Crow Community College, put it this way: "Our language speaks to us and reveals to us our philosophies. We just have to start listening again."

However, as fluent Native language speakers continue to age and pass on, revitalization becomes a race against time. "Figuratively speaking, the language waters are still ten feet deep so we can immerse ourselves in the resources we have," says Ho-

Chunk instructor Elaine Rice in the article "Little Priest Tribal College Immerses Students in Language." But she warns, "In a few years, if we do nothing, our fluency—our resources—may be too shallow to allow us to have these classes."

The challenges are myriad and great. Learning an Indigenous language, especially for those whose first language is English, can be a daunting, difficult, and painstaking process. It's fundamentally different than learning other Indo-European languages such as Spanish or French because Native languages are members of linguistic families that have their own unique rules and structures. Some linguists and language instructors at tribal colleges maintain that it takes a language learner about 2,000 hours of listening before she will understand 95% of the language. After 6,000 hours, one becomes functionally bilingual, and at 12,000 hours, she's a fluent speaker. To put those numbers into perspective, it takes approximately 5,760 hours of time spent in the classroom to complete a baccalaureate degree. That's a significant time commitment, especially for students with families and jobs.

Due to the complexity of language revitalization, it is a multifaceted endeavor. All tribal colleges offer language classes and most require at least a class or two as part of students' general education coursework. But Indigenous language revitalization also necessitates a unique curriculum and teaching methods. Native languages often lack textbooks, dictionaries, and other instructional materials. And when the resources do exist, they need to be carefully reviewed and updated, as many were developed by non-Native academics or missionaries who harbored a distinctly non-Native perspective. Due to these limitations, tribal colleges have often had to strike out on their own, into an unknown pedagogical and curricular frontier.

Fortunately, tribal communities have their own precious resources that have helped maintain and energize language revitalization. Elders and community members are at the fore of the process and have proved to be linchpins upon which both preservation and revitalization hinge. They have brought refreshingly new teaching strategies that bridge the language-culture divide and embody active learning. At most tribal colleges, student language learners are not tied to their seats, passively receiving information. They are engaged, participatory, hands-on, active.

Still, there are limitations to learning language in the classroom. One may develop an impressive vocabulary and fully understand the syntax and every grammatical rule, but still find the language unintelligible when he hears it. This has been the case with more than just a handful of students who have taken language classes. "I was one of those individuals who had taken every language course offered locally and . . . after about 10 years of studying the language, I got so proficient in grammar that I developed three grammar courses," recalls Ted Holappa from Bay Mills Community College. "But I still couldn't understand what a fluent speaker was saying to me, let alone engage in a conversation beyond the basics. I was very frustrated and wondered if maybe I wasn't working hard enough, or maybe I wasn't smart enough." Holappa, like many students earnestly seeking fluency in their Native language, came to realize he had to seek out another route, concluding, "You can't memorize this language word by word. You have to be here immersed in the program where the language is washing over you."

Today, immersion is considered the best way to learn a second language and tribal colleges have taken note. They have developed a multitude of cutting-edge immersion projects, including language nests, daycares, preschools, primary schools, charter schools, retreats, and camps. While each project may target a specific age demographic, all rest on the philosophy that language is not learned, but rather it is acquired. Compared with other methods, language immersion produces fluent speakers in relatively short periods of time, as students can accumulate hours of time in concentrated intervals.

Language revitalization, whether carried out in classrooms or immersion projects, remains one of the most important missions for tribal colleges and universities because the vitality of Indian peoples correlates directly to the vitality of their languages. In an effort to contribute to our understanding of the past, present, and future of language revitalization, *Tribal College Journal* (TCJ) has compiled this volume to chronicle how TCUs have pioneered efforts in the field. Most of the articles here have been previously published, either in TCJ or other publications. All focus on tribal colleges and examine their efforts.

This book consists of four main sections, and the articles in each are organized chronologically to illuminate how language revitalization efforts have transformed and evolved over time. The first section, entitled "Overviews," contains three articles that assess the state of language preservation and revitalization at a particular point in time. Each piece looks at language revitalization efforts broadly, while using programming at specific TCUs to illustrate important trends or developments. The second section, "Voices," consists of essays that showcase various perspectives and philosophies on language revitalization. Many of the authors offer diverging opinions or posit new possible strategies; all, however, concur on the great importance of the overall TCU effort. The third section, "Profiles," gives readers an in-depth look at revitalization efforts at specific tribal colleges over the past quarter century. Indeed, TCJ itself was founded in part for the tribal colleges to share information so that they can learn from one another. Each of these program profiles does just that, enabling educators to discover varying strategies and resources. The last section consists of a comprehensive research study that was commissioned by the American Indian College Fund and published independently. Authored by longtime TCU leader and educator, Janine Pease, the study offers a thorough analysis of language immersion projects at TCUs and beyond.

The educators and activists leading the effort to revitalize Native languages are faced with a great challenge, but it is not insurmountable. If there is one thing that American Indian peoples have proven repeatedly, it is their resiliency. It is our hope that this volume will contribute to and help inform those efforts.

OVERVIEWS

Tribal colleges and universities have played a central role in the evolution of Indigenous language revitalization in the United States and Canada. Not only have they initiated new methods and curricula, but they have also developed resources and teaching materials that can be used in language courses. Tribally chartered, owned, and controlled, TCUs have taken the initiative to utilize elders, community members, Indigenous ways of knowing, and other cultural resources that are unavailable to other institutions. In this regard, they are better positioned to preserve and revitalize Native languages than any other school, college, university, or organization. In the three articles that follow, readers can take a bird's eye view of the state of language revitalization at tribal colleges at the time in which each article was written.

Janine Pease's summary, "New Voices, Ancient Words: Language Immersion Produces Fluent Speakers, Stronger Personal and Cultural Identities," published in spring 2004 issue of *Tribal College Journal,* is a distillation of a comprehensive research study commissioned by the American Indian College Fund (the full study can be found in the Research section of this book). Pease investigated pioneering immersion programs in New Zealand and Hawaii, giving special attention to who taught language courses, how they prepared classes, the sources of support, and the role that elders, parents, and other community members played in the classroom. Her study proved especially useful for TCUs, who could replicate aspects of these immersion efforts they deemed applicable or useful.

Seven years after Pease's article, the American Indian Higher Education Consortium commissioned former TCJ editor Paul Boyer to write "Native Languages and Tribally Controlled Colleges: Giving Voice to Native Nations," a heretofore unpublished report on the state of language revitalization at tribal colleges. Boyer looks broadly at the teaching of Indigenous languages, reaching back to the boarding school era when missionaries and other educators embraced an English-only curriculum that sought to assimilate Native peoples. Their efforts proved terribly destructive, making modern revitalization efforts all the more difficult. Nevertheless, TCUs have made remarkable progress and implemented strategies to reclaim their Indigenous languages. Boyer recognizes that fluency is often fleeting, but maintains that the pride and cultural renewal that Indigenous language instruction brings to tribal communities has great value in and of itself.

Laura Paskus, also a former editor of TCJ, rounds out this section with her essay, "More than Words, a Way of Life: Language Restoration Programs Reach Beyond Tribal Colleges and Universities." Paskus' overview appeared as one of the feature articles in TCJ's summer 2013 issue devoted to language revitalization. Paskus looks at a handful of tribal colleges, including Aaniiih Nakoda College, Oglala Lakota College, and Iḷisaġvik College, and investigates the intersection of culture and language in various immersion programs. She reveals the undergirding philosophy behind many of these efforts, perhaps best articulated by Tom Raymond, Oglala Lakota College's dean of education and the principal of the college's K-4 immersion school, who states, "You don't just learn a language, you learn a way of living. It reflects back on the old ways of life, when there was a lot of sharing, and traditional ways of living. I'm not talking about dancing back the buffalo, and everyone's wearing feathers and skins and lives in tipis. I'm talking about preserving a traditional way of life that is one with the world around."

New Voices, Ancient Words
Language Immersion Produces Fluent Speakers, Stronger Personal and Cultural Identities

By Janine Pease

Across Indian Country, you can hear their voices, young voices speaking ancient words—in a Cochiti extended family in New Mexico, a Navajo community school in the Arizona desert, a Native Hawaiian kindergarten, a Salish-Kootenai summertime ceremony, on the North Dakota plains, and in a Blackfeet math classroom in Montana. It is called Native language immersion, and it represents a revolution in Native American education. Language immersion not only increases fluency and promises the survival of threatened languages and cultures. It also may reverse dismal student test scores and restore fractured families and communities.

Two years ago, the W.K. Kellogg Foundation commissioned research on Native language immersion; the American Indian College Fund administered the project. The study looked at the different approaches taken by Indigenous people in this country and New Zealand.[1] What does language immersion look like? Who are the students? Who are the teachers, and how are they prepared? How does language immersion involve tribal elders and parents? What resources support it?

The literature review included 43 sources, with an emphasis on works by Native American educators and linguists. Interviews were conducted with language immersion practitioners, parents, elders, and planners of many tribes, including Blackfeet, Crow, Ojibwa, Assiniboine, Ute, Salish, Hidatsa, and Pueblo, as well as Maori People of New Zealand and Native Hawaiians.

---

[1] See Pease, "Native American Language Immersion: Innovative Native Education for Children and Families," pp. 153-215.

"New Voices, Ancient Words: Language Immersion Produces Fluent Speakers, Stronger Personal and Cultural Identities" appeared in *Tribal College: Journal of American Indian Higher Education, 15*(4), in spring 2004.

4 | OVERVIEWS

What Is Language Immersion?

Unlike other language instruction methods, language immersion follows the learning path an infant takes on the way to fluency in a primary language. It concentrates on communication. The child or participant spends all of the day in the tribal language; most sites have a "no English" rule. The students know English, of course. In most cases, students have been raised in English-speaking homes and are immersed in English constantly outside of the classroom. Learning activities utilize traditional Native ways of knowing and learning: highly interactive, hands-on exploration and discovery, observation, and listening. Students learn language within the context of each tribal culture, and thus no two programs are alike.

It's quite important to understand what language immersion is not. It is not: lists of vocabulary words to memorize and phrases to translate; 40-minute classes five times a week; word searches in a two-way dictionary; digression into English to explain a word or phrase; drills in the structure of the language, like conjugation of verbs. Participants think and speak in the Native language, without translation time delays. The Native language is not a "subject" but the medium through which all subjects are instructed. Math, science, art, and music are taught in languages such as Blackfeet or Native Hawaiian. The Native language is the language of learning, interactions, and all communications.

Although Native people learned languages of their own and neighboring tribes by immersion for hundreds of years, their use of immersion as a technique for revitalizing Native languages began fairly recently. Fewer than 50 have more than three years of sustained programming. These include the Indigenous Maori people of New Zealand and the Native Hawaiians (who started their schools more than 20 years ago), and a few with 15 or more years of operation such as Akwesasne Freedom School of the Mohawk Nation in New York and the Piegan Institute of the Blackfeet Nation in Montana. The Piegan Institute started preschool immersion in 1995 and started the *Nizipuhwahsin*

(Real Speak) School four years later; today they have three K-8 schools.

Instructors and activists are from all walks of life, from bus drivers to retired Bureau of Indian Affairs professionals. Although few are professional educators, they combine their knowledge of traditional learning with language teaching methods. Their passion for language and culture feeds their commitment.

Why Language Immersion?

What motivates these language activists? What compels them to do this work? Compared with other methods, language immersion produces fluent speakers in relatively short periods of time. More is at stake than just the languages, however. The vitality of the language ties directly to the vitality and well being of the people. Research shows that immersion improves overall educational achievement, strengthens family ties, and increases retention rates, keeping Native students in school who might otherwise drop out. Finally, some activists engage in this difficult work because of its potential to allay centuries of subjugation.

The research on Native American students in English-speaking public schools shows dismal educational achievement. In many states in 2000-2001, the high school completion rate for American Indian students was lower than 70% (e.g., 45% in Minnesota, 46% in Nebraska, 58% in North Dakota, and 42% in South Dakota), according to the National Center for Education Statistics. Recent data from the U.S. Department of Education show American Indians' test scores far below white students' in all subjects. For example, 90% of American Indian students were below proficient in math in 2000 as compared with 66% of white students.

In contrast, language immersion students demonstrate remarkable achievement in all subjects on standardized tests. Research has documented such results at Blackfeet, Native Hawaiian, Navajo Rough Rock and Rock Point, and Maori language immersion schools. Students at Piegan Institute's *Nizipuhwahsin* (Real Speak) School in Montana—who have been taught all subjects in their Native languages K-8—out perform their public school counterparts in standardized test scores administered in English.

Native Hawaiians who have been in immersion school from preschool through high school have gone on to highly competitive institutions like Stanford and Oxford. New Zealand youth take exit tests, similar to the European secondary systems, in order to graduate. In 1975 (when all instruction was in English), the high school graduation rates for Maori students at Wharekura o Rakamanga were only 15%, but the Maori immersion school changed that 15% to an astounding 75% in 2002. These 2002 Maori graduates had been in immersion schools all their lives. This school in a low-income, majority Maori neighborhood had not only retained its students, but the students demonstrated their educational achievement—also on standardized tests administered in English.

As students study their Native language and culture, they develop stronger identities and knowledge of their individual roles in their culture and family. Every program requires the commitment of students' parents, thereby strengthening the Native families. Students also develop intergenerational relationships with other elders and traditional resource people, thereby strengthening the entire community. The language carries with it the knowledge of relationships, and the language learners acquire a sense of these connections.

How Is It Taught?

The practitioners are creating their own combination of methods that capitalize upon their communities' and their own individual strengths. While one might teach language using the stars, another will build rawhide shields, and yet another will spend a day exploring a sacred spring. Youthful instructors might choose total physical movement; grandmothers and grandfathers might profile a chief and teach about leadership. Immersion is by definition highly innovative, without rules. The projects in this study utilized three primary language immersion methods, the

"Grandparents' Method," total physical response, and/or Montessori.

Grandparents are the traditional teachers of Indian children, and language immersion projects draw upon tribal elders' expertise in a multitude of ways. These elders are not only fluent in the language, but they also share their extensive knowledge of tribal oral literature, history, and the sciences. They know and interact with the tribal sacred places. With the grandparents' method, students learn by participating in daily activities, seasonal traditions, artistry, and storytelling, according to Darrell Kipp (Blackfeet), one of the founders of the Piegan Institute. This method immerses the student in not only the language but also the culture.

Total physical response (TPR) is a new term for an age-old, effective method of language acquisition. James Asher popularized TPR for language acquisition in the 1960s and 1970s. Learners respond physically to simple requests by the teacher, who uses gestures to get across the instructions. Acting out the requested behaviors helps students remember the new phrases. Initially silent, the students gradually learn to ask other students to perform actions, recombining vocabulary to make new requests. Many of the tribal language immersion educators/activists have adopted this method, focusing on singing, games, storytelling, and other group activities. Especially useful with second language learning, it provides students with the opportunity to recognize fairly sizeable and useful vocabularies in a relatively short time period; within four to five weeks, students learn to recognize 150 words or more, according to Jon Reyhner of Northern Arizona University.

Montessori schools organize the learning environment around "interest islands," and learning activities follow the interest level of each child among the islands. Several Native American language immersion preschools have adapted this method by installing tribal knowledge and cultural resources in the interest islands. Because the method makes no pre-supposition on learning content or context, Native language educators choose it for its similarity to the grandparents' way of teaching and its adaptability to tribal specific language and culture, according to Carol Baker-Olguin, director of the Southern Ute Indian Academy.

Language immersion requires human interaction; thus few of the projects in this study utilize technology. Language immersion practitioners vary greatly in their attitudes toward it. Writing about the *Sm'algyax* language renewal, Daniel Rubin has reported that computer-assisted instruction, such as audio and video clips, can be an important supplement for today's students. In settings where the tribal language is in critical condition and the number of fluent speakers limited, technology can provide "life support," according to Dr. Richard Littlebear (Northern Cheyenne). On the other hand, Kipp of the Blackfeet Tribe, says, "Technology is a waste of precious resources, a trade-off for real time and applied teaching and learning, directly with children."

Where Is It Taught?

Preschools, daycare centers, and "language nests" are among the most impressive language immersion projects in Native America. The learning environment most frequently chosen for the "language nest" is a grandma's home. The learning activities follow the daily routine of living, utilizing the tribal language (no English). In several locations, the language immersion activists have begun with preschools and developed them into schools, adding one grade level at a time. For example, the Piegan Institute started preschool immersion in 1995; today they have three K-8 schools. In addition, the Lac Courte Oreilles Ojibwa of Wisconsin, the Cochiti Pueblo of New Mexico, the Diné of Arizona, and the Onondaga of New York all have developed elementary immersion schools.

Many tribal groups adopt a camp as the first step in immersion learning. They provide short-term, time-concentrated learning opportunities where participants can follow the seasonal cycles and learn language in the context of their culture. Native people of all ages experience tribal oral literature, history, arts, music, and natural resources in the outdoors environment. Camp directors usually have camps on tribal lands chosen for the richest language learning potential. The learning teams organize around an educator/activist to explore, discuss, discover, and experience. Teams adopt Native family attributes, especially those of relationship and group learning.

The mentor/apprentice language immersion programs are among the most innovative in Indian Country. Organizers match masters of the tribal language and culture with apprentices for long-term learning relationships patterned after Native tradition. The Three Affiliated Tribes of North Dakota have a mentor project that joins one master with five apprentices for a multiple year period of language and culture learning, entirely situated in the tribal community. Alongside the master, the apprentices acquire the languages through the arts, songs, ceremonies, and living history of the tribes. The apprentices enroll in the tribal language major at the Fort Berthold Community College[2] as teacher trainees and teach one of the three languages (Hidatsa, Arikara, or Mandan) half time in the local schools. Thus this project cascades with a ripple effect from the master, to the apprentice, to the school children, and back into the community, according to Clarice Baker Big Back (Hidatsa/Mandan), administrator of the program and vice president at Fort Berthold Community College.

Each Dakota language master works with an entire family at Lake Andes on the Yankton Indian Reservation in South Dakota. The project staff supports the relationship between the mentor and the family members (mom, dad, and children). This especially creative approach utilizes the strength of family relationships to promote language learning in homes, following a schedule of traditional activities.

What Lies in the Future?

Language immersion organizers and activists face many challenges. First, to be effective, they must commit to this difficult work for the long term. Second, fluent language speakers are often the eldest members of a tribal community; sometimes age and

---

[2] Fort Berthold Community College changed its name to Nueta Hidatsa Sahnish College in 2015.

health make it difficult for them to participate in physically demanding activities. Third, the experiential and group learning methods necessary for language immersion require more complex planning and organization than standard classroom instruction. Fourth, many tribal community members harbor negative feelings about education and learning of any kind based on their personal and tribal histories. Finally, while initial funding for language immersion may be available (from public and private sources), sustained support is hard to acquire; language immersion must be sustained for many years to be effective. Tribes find it difficult to fund language programs when they have so many serious social and economic needs.

For millennia, Native people have taught their children for living and living well. It is still done today. In a growing number of Native communities, one can hear people young and old speaking Blackfeet, Diné, Keresan, Hidatsa, Dakota, Salish, and Ojibwa. The revolution has a voice.

Janine Pease, EdD (Crow), served as president of Little Big Horn College, where she played a major role in the tribal languages collaborative among Montana tribal colleges, the Learning Lodge Institute.

Native Languages and Tribally Controlled Colleges
Giving Voice to Native Nations

By Paul Boyer

Two Stories

As a small child, Selena Ditmar spoke Nakoda, the language of the Assiniboine people living on the Fort Belknap reservation of northern Montana. She was not alone. Most of her relatives and neighbors were fluent in the language of their ancestors. "My family all spoke it," she recalled.

In time she went off to the local public school, along with her older sister. On her first day, she could not understand the teacher, or the non-Indian children. But she was a fast learner. Quickly, and with little difficulty, she became bilingual. Before long, she could speak both Nakoda—the language of her people and her heritage—and English, the language of the dominant society. Eventually, she became a nurse, married, and had children of her own. She used English at work and Nakoda at home and with her relatives. Each had its place and value.

By the early 1960s, however, Selena noticed that English was spoken more and more frequently within the reservation. Like a small breach in a large dam, no one was alarmed; from one day to the next, life went on as before. Nakoda remained a vital part of daily communication—until, suddenly, it wasn't. By the early 1990s Selena looked around and realized that only a small and rapidly shrinking pool of elders still spoke Nakoda with confidence. The rest of the tribe spoke only English. Even her own children had failed to master the language. Her grandchildren were monolingual.

Selena lives in a cozy and spotless home at the end of a long dirt drive, just off Route 2—the famed Montana Highline—which

---

"Native Languages and Tribally Controlled Colleges: Giving Voice to Native Nations" was a report commissioned by the American Indian Higher Education Consortium in 2011.

runs parallel with the Canadian border. In this rural region of rolling grasslands and rugged hills populated by small and scattered towns, she estimated that there are only five or six fluent tribal members who can carry on conversations in her language. "I have no one to speak to now," she said. To keep from forgetting the language, she speaks to herself. Sometimes she cannot remember a word and must wait a day or two until it comes back to her; there is no one to ask.

As a girl, Selena liked going to the movies, and enjoyed watching Westerns. She remembered that she always rooted for the cowboys and cheered when they beat the Indians. She laughs and shakes her head. Now she would like to see young tribal members go out into the world proud of their Native identity. Language, she suggested, is at the heart of this effort.

***

A half day's drive south is the heart of the Northern Cheyenne reservation and the campus of Chief Dull Knife College (CDKC). The small tribal college occupies an assortment of mismatched buildings in the center of Lame Deer and is easily overlooked by the passerby. But once inside the main administration building, visitors are warmly greeted by Bryaira Pryor, one of the college's 200 students. When not in class, she works at the reception desk, answering phones, directing visitors—and practicing her Northern Cheyenne.

On a recent day just before the end of the spring term, she had written *Mešeneo'o ešeamevonehneo'o* on a white board by the office door. In English the word means "Ticks are crawling." Bryaira explains that "ticks" are wood ticks and that they come out when winter ends. Like crocuses or robins, it's a traditional sign of spring, and an event noted by elders. Bryaira just learned this phrase. At 27, she is working to learn the Northern Cheyenne so she can help pass it on to her young children.

Bryaira was raised by her grandmother, a fluent speaker of her tribe's language. But like many of her generation, her parents and grandparents did not teach her the language. "Grandkids, great grandkids—none of us knew the Northern Cheyenne language," she said. In Head Start and elementary school, she was exposed to a few Northern Cheyenne words and phrases. However, these brief encounters with the language were not enough to build anything approaching fluency.

As a teenager, Bryaira regretted losing this connection to her heritage and language. She found some instructional material online and tried—without success—to teach herself. This happened while she was living off the reservation with her father. Far away from other Northern Cheyenne speakers, she couldn't practice or stay motivated.

Now that she is back home and the mother of three small children, she is filled with renewed determination. When the college started a daycare program in 2011 with a Northern Cheyenne language focus she eagerly enrolled her two youngest daughters. As part of this unique program, parents are also provided six hours of formal language instruction a week. Bryaira ruefully notes that her daughters are learning the language faster than she is, but she is not daunted. "My goal is to keep up with the language so it doesn't fade away in my family." She wants to speak Northern Cheyenne to her children, and she wants her children to be able to speak to their elders.

"That's one thing I really, really want," she says, pausing as her eyes brim with tears. "Especially being my grandmother's great grandchildren...." Filled with a sudden rush of emotion, her voice catches and she trails off, looking for the right way to explain her feelings. But nothing more need be said. Already, the fullness of her longing and her hope is expressed. The power and importance of the Northern Cheyenne language is explained not in grammar, politics, or policy. It is revealed in the small words that might some day be shared between a little girl and a great grandmother.

The Resiliency of Native Languages

All tribal languages are threatened. Many have disappeared from daily use, and nearly all are endangered. It is tempting to assume that this reflects a sad but inevitable evolution in Indian societies. Nakota, Crow, Northern Cheyenne—among dozens of other languages—are simply part of the past. They cannot be saved and, nostalgia aside, have lost their utility.

But the larger story of Native languages in the 21st century is richer and more complex. Native languages remain an important and powerful part of most tribal communities. Even in the era of television, high speed internet, Facebook, and Twitter, it is possible to hear Navajo on AM radio and Crow in tribal council deliberations. Children's books are published in Salish and Iñupiaq can be learned through Rosetta Stone. Jokes are still told in Tewa and songs are sung in Lakota. After 500 years of colonization and sustained efforts to separate Indians from their heritage, more than 169 distinct tribal languages survive in the United States and are spoken by an estimated 237,000 people, according to a 2011 U.S. Census report. Most are clustered in the Southwest, but speakers are found from coast to coast, and from the Arctic Circle to the Mexican border.

These languages survive because they have value. They are not relics of the past, but an important part of modern tribal life and are essential for the growth and well-being of Native communities. By sustaining their languages, tribes are able to maintain their place as distinctive peoples within the dominant society. "It identifies us as who we are," Selena Ditmar asserted. Indeed, languages are the "largest part" of a society's cultural identity according to noted linguist David Crystal. More subtly, language also affirms social bonds and, many believe, help restore a sense of personal identity and individual pride that, when lost, too easily leads to alcoholism, drug use, and other social ills.

The possible loss of language in many reservations does not lead to complacency. As the stories of Selena Ditmar and Bryaira Pryor powerfully demonstrate, it inspires alarm and calls to action. Tribal members are fighting, and fighting hard, to retain language fluency where it exists and restore this essential part of their identity where it teeters on the brink. For many, language survival is one of the most pressing and urgent tasks facing tribal nations.

The Role of Tribal Colleges

In this effort, tribally controlled colleges and universities (TCUs) have an especially important role to play. These institutions, which in most cases are located on reservations, have a unique mission to serve the academic, social, and cultural needs of their tribal nations. Their commitment to culturally grounded instruction and community renewal means that most have also made language survival a priority. Most teach the language of their tribe; many require one or more semesters of language study in order to meet general education requirements. They are often the only institutions in the world where their language is formally taught.

In recent years, these colleges have made language survival an even higher priority. Concerned about accelerating language loss, TCUs are emerging as centers for scholarship, curriculum development, and advocacy. They are training elementary school language teachers; working with elders and professional linguists to compile accurate dictionaries and grammar guides; and purposefully incorporating the language into student life and formal college events, such as graduation ceremonies. All this helps elevate the visibility and credibility of the language.

Some colleges are doing even more. The newest and most significant trend is the development of language camps, daycare programs, and even comprehensive K-8 language immersion schools. These are often large and costly efforts, but many feel language survival depends on teaching language in childhood and providing language-centered instruction during all years of schooling.

This work represents a significant commitment from the tribal colleges. Most are small institutions and all are poor relative to their mainstream counterparts. Yet funding for research, curriculum development, and instruction is limited. In 2011, for example, federal funding for Native American language preservation and maintenance through the Administration for Native Americans totaled only $3 million and funded only 12 projects. Private sector grants from small advocacy organizations and foundations provide important support to a wider group of scholars and tribes, but cannot fill the gap. As a result, much of the work described here is supported by colleges out their general funds and, in the case of instructors, out of their own pockets.

The value of the work is reflected in the college's commitment, despite a lack of resources. To succeed, however, the colleges must overcome a century of federal Indian policy and the more subtle contemporary influence of poverty, low expectations, and a pervasive mass media.

The Struggle for Survival

The first sustained threat to Native languages in the United States began with the founding of government and missionary boarding schools in the 19th century. In this era of forced assimilation, it was widely believed that Native languages were a barrier to the civilization of Indian children and should be replaced by English as quickly as possible. "[T]he instruction of Indians in the vernacular [tribal language] is not only of no use to them," wrote U.S. Commissioner of Indian Affairs J.D.C. Atkins in the mid-1880s, "but is detrimental to the cause of their education and civilization and it will not be permitted in any Indian school over which the government has any control."

What most clearly marked the harshness of this era, however, was the contempt expressed toward Native languages and the active suppression of its use. It was not enough for students to learn a new language; they must forget and even renounce their own language. Native languages were banned—not only from classrooms, but also from all private conversation. Those who violated this rule risked punishment, including beatings. Former students recall meeting in secret to share a few words, always fearful of discovery.

This policy softened in later decades, particularly in the 1930s and 1940s, during the Roosevelt administration's Indian New Deal. But the underlying attitude that Native languages were inferior—"barbarous" was the term used by Commissioner Atkins—and a barrier to their education remained deeply entrenched in boarding, missionary, and public schools into the mid-20th century. Today, many adults have painful memories of their first days in school when they encountered both an alien language and unsympathetic teachers.

At the same time, many tribal members also internalized the deeper message repeated by teachers and government agents that Native languages were inferior and without value in modern society. "My grandparents never spoke the language because it wasn't right in their day," recalled Carole Falcon-Chandler, president of Aaniiih Nakoda College (ANC), which serves the Fort Belknap reservation. "It wasn't accepted." Although her grandmother was a fluent speaker of Aaniiih (also widely known as Gros Ventre), none of 10 children learned the language.

Hubert Two Leggins Remembers His First Day of School

Hubert Two Leggings vividly remembers his first day of school. He arrived at the local elementary school, which served both the Crow tribe and surrounding non-Indian communities, fluent only in the tribal language. Everything was new and he couldn't understand a word spoken by his non-Indian teacher.

When the children went outside for recess, he and the other Crow boys followed. They gravitated to the edge of a paved playground, where they started playing in the dirt, as they so often did at home. It was a familiar and reassuring activity.

Suddenly, the teacher appeared, clearly angry. The Indian boys were taken back inside, lined up, and made to hold out their hands. A thick wooden yardstick appeared and the teacher loudly slapped the palms of the first boy's hands. "He screamed and cried," Two Leggings recalled. "We all screamed and cried." He did not know why the teacher was hitting him. For all the children, it was scene of pain and confusion.

Only later did he learn that the teacher had told the children before recess—in a language he did not understand—not to leave the pavement or play in the dirt. "That was my first day at school," he said.

Two Leggings was not punished for speaking Crow. But he was ultimately being punished for not arriving at school already fluent in English. Many similar experiences help explain why so many young tribal members on the Crow reservation and elsewhere report that their parents or grandparents refused to teach them the tribal language. Adults wanted to protect their children from such painful experiences. They hoped that by emphasizing English in the home their children would not feel confusion or shame when they went off to school.

Boarding schools and uncompromising assimilationist policies were then doubly destructive. They not only disrupted use of Native languages within schools, they also triggered a self-imposed censorship of these languages within homes and tribal communities. Out of love and concern, parents tried to protect their children by using English and refusing to speak their own language. Hoping for a brighter future, they embraced the language of mainstream society and came to view their language with shame more than pride. This internally imposed silence rippled across Native communities into the next generation—and the generations beyond.

Today, few boarding schools remain, and those that exist often celebrate Native language and culture. Many public schools, which now serve the vast majority of Indian students, are also more respectful of Indian cultures and some even teach the language of the local tribe. Ironically, some Indian children first encounter their own language in local public schools, not the home, although instruction is usually limited to a few words and phrases.

These are positive changes, yet new challenges have emerged in the modern era. At the top of the list, most agree, is the pervasive influence of mainstream media—television and radio, as well as growing role of the internet and social media. While access to this technology is often useful and empowering for tribes, its presence is a double-edged sword. Professional linguists call English the "language killer" because of its tendency to simply overwhelm local languages wherever it is introduced. And through television and the internet, English now rushes into the homes of even the most geographically isolated reservations. Even before they start school, many young tribal members are more versed in pop culture colloquialisms than traditional words or ancient stories.

Greater mobility also weakens languages. In the 1940s, for example, many young men left for military service. In more recent years, tribal members leave for careers, college, or because of marriage to non-tribal members. This sense of opportunity and free choice is welcome, of course, but language skills often deteriorate away from home and, most critically, children who are raised off the reservation are much less likely to learn the language—even when parents make the effort.

Lark Real Bird exemplifies the challenge of language survival when living away from the tribal community. She grew up on the Crow reservation and now teaches both art and the Crow language at Little Big Horn College (LBHC). But her husband is not a member of the tribe and, significantly, her children spent their first years off the reservation while she was completing her graduate degree. Although she is deeply committed to the survival of her language, none of her children speak Crow. "I work with them a lot," she said, noting that her oldest son, now a teenager, can understand the language—but still won't speak it. Similar stories are told across Indian Country by young tribal members who are well educated and deeply committed to their language and Native identity—yet struggle to pass on the language within their own families.

Finally, tribal members point to one final barrier: a lack awareness and action within tribes. Linguists frequently report that Native communities often fail to understand that their language is slipping away until it is almost too late. The warning signs are often missed because change happens relatively slowly in the context of an individual's life. But even when the impending loss is finally understood, community leaders are often slow to respond. Members may not feel qualified to take action or believe the crisis will be addressed by unseen experts. Internal debates—over emotionally charged issues related to writing systems or vocabulary—also sap energy.

Inaction also results from the difficulty of learning a second language. Contrary to popular belief, Native languages are not "simple." In fact, they are notoriously difficult to learn. With rich vocabularies and distinctive, complex grammars, they can quickly discourage casual language learners. Sean Chandler, director of the American Indian studies program at ANC, explained with a mixture of amusement and exasperation that tribal members often express interest in the Aaniiih language and ask for a copy of a dictionary compiled by a linguist in the 1980s. But once they page through the thick tome, "they realize the mountain you have to climb and they put it on the shelf."

The barriers facing tribes are significant. They must overcome more than 150 years of forced assimilation and government policies that weakened the use of, and respect for, hundreds of ancient languages. In addition, language advocates must push against the modern forces of acculturation and inaction within communities. Faced with these obstacles, it is easy to question the value of maintaining languages. In modern tribal societies where English is already the *lingua franca*, why bother to maintain, save, or even restore a language? Does a language, spoken by a small community of people, have a viable role to play in modern American society?

Tribal leaders say it does. In fact, they assert that language survival is an essential part of a larger effort to build strong, self-reliant communities. Their work is guided not by nostalgia or a rejection of contemporary life, but by an understanding that language survival is directly linked to social renewal, economic development, and academic achievement. Many believe it is one of the most urgent tasks facing tribes in the 21st century.

Why Languages Matter

By the late 1960s it was clear that Indians had not assimilated into mainstream society, despite centuries of effort by European colonists and the American government. They still existed as separate people and as a distinctive culture. But it was also clear that the unrelenting pursuit of assimilation had left a vast landscape of poverty, dependency, and social fragmentation. In this era of protest and social reform, a cadre of young tribal members rejected government control of Indian communities and offered a different strategy: They believed tribes should take charge of their own development and rebuild pride in their Native identities. The future depended upon building, not destroying, tribal nations and embracing, not rejecting, cultural traditions. The goal was not assimilation, but tribal self-determination.

The movement grew slowly, but over the past 40 years, radical changes have taken place. Many tribes have reasserted control over their governments, established their own economic develop policies, and begun building their own education systems. And through these systems, they have worked to restore a sense of nationhood. Tribes are exerting their right and responsibility to act as sovereign nations.

In this context, language has important roles to play because it is through language that nations are able to maintain cohesive and self-aware societies, distinct from all others. This is true for all nations, but it is especially important for tribes, which must exist within the much larger boundaries of American society. Against forces that weaken local communities, languages allow tribal peoples to be "inward looking, but in the best sense," according to linguist David Crystal, by "fostering family ties, maintaining social relations, giving people a sense of their 'pedigree.'" The dominant language, he concludes, "cannot do this."

In this way, language survival is part of a larger social and political movement to strengthen tribal nations. However, it is also clear that languages are, for many tribal members, valued at an even deeper and more emotional level. Across Indian Country, many explain that language renewal is part of a personal reawakening, a search for identity as a Native person. For many, the task of learning and speaking an ancestral language expresses a strongly felt desire to capture a sense of purpose and personal pride that past assimilationist policies weakened and derided. Tribal members—men and women both—are often brought to tears when talking about the loss and recovery of their own languages.

It's about "self-esteem, [being a] self-confident person, doing better," summarized ANC President Carole Falcon-Chandler. While she was not taught the language, she watched with pride as her own son and daughter-in-law set out to relearn the language on their own. They succeeded and are now passing the language on to her grandchildren. She understands how empowering it can be. "I know a few little openings when I'm speaking at graduation," she said. "It just makes me feel so good when I can do that and I wish I could do more."

Burt Medicine Bull on the Importance of Language Revitalization

Northern Cheyenne language instructor Burt Medicine Bull does not hesitate when asked why tribal members should learn their language. It's all about "pride and identity," he said. The act of learning Northern Cheyenne builds a connection to his tribe's heritage, the community, and to each other. "It heals them," he said. "There is a lot of healing that takes place."

Medicine Bull currently teaches at Chief Dull Knife College, but he started out teaching at the local elementary school. He understands that some students—especially young children—lack interest in their language, in part because they feel ashamed of their Indian identity. In response, he often began his elementary school courses by talking about the tribe's past, about its struggle for survival during the nineteenth century when the tribe endured starvation, relocations, and the killing of women and children by American soldiers.

Most powerfully, he would tell his students about personally witnessing the repatriation of skeletal remains taken by the United States government in the late 19th century and kept for decades by the Smithsonian Institution in Washington, D.C. Among those returned to the tribe in 1993 for reburial through the Native American Graves Protection and Repatriation Act was a small box containing the remains of a four-year-old girl. She had a bullet wound through the head.

The children listened, and "after midterm, they all were talking the language, Medicine Bull said. "I saw the transformation. They were proud. They were no longer on the outside looking in. They were proud; they belonged."

With this pride, say tribal leaders, comes a new respect for tribal values and a determination to build stronger tribal nations. It is well known that many reservations are besieged by alcoholism, domestic violence, political in-fighting, and related social ills. But tribal leaders emphasize that these are modern pathologies, not traditional tribal practices. The future, they argue, depends on recapturing an older set of values based on respect, generosity, and courtesy. Language offers a path of social renewal because these values are actually embedded in the vocabulary and grammar of their native tongues. Sean Chandler noted for example that the Aaniiih word for leader is not "chief," but "generous person." Bravery mattered, he said, but if you cared for the orphaned or the elderly, "people thought a lot of you." These are the qualities of leadership that the tribe must restore and celebrate, he suggested.

Finally, tribal languages matter because they actually promote higher academic achievement. This might sound counterintuitive. Isn't it better to come to school speaking English, as generations of government agents and non-Indian educators assumed? But the problem, according to experienced teachers, is that too many students lack fluency in any language. Many children continue to grow up in homes where the tribal language is largely lost, yet English is not spoken fluently or correctly. As a result, children come to school speaking only a kind of "slang English" that inhibits learning, according to Lark Real Bird at LBHC.

Without a strong foundation in either language, students struggle in all subjects, from history and art to math and science. "I can't teach them in Crow and I can't teach them in English," summarized Loretta Three Irons, a retired elementary school teacher on the Crow reservation. This observation is supported by a large body of research. The conclusive finding is that children who arrive in school fluent in a tribal language are better equipped to master English and succeed academically than students who are semi-fluent in two languages. And when students become bilingual, they are doubly enriched: A growing body of research finds that knowing a second language improves cognitive function and strengthens the learning process (de Lang, 31).

For all of these reasons, tribal leaders agree that language survival and renewal is a top priority for the health and well-being of their nations. Until recently, however, many communities lacked the resources and expertise needed to raise awareness, provide instruction, and encourage the active use of language in the community—which are all necessary steps if a language is to remain a vibrant part of a tribal community. Fortunately, TCUs are stepping up to the challenge. Their unique commitment to community-based education and social renewal means that language survival is a growing priority for these small but vibrant institutions of higher learning.

The Vital Role of Tribally Controlled Colleges

Although tribally controlled colleges are small and under-funded institutions, they are leaders in the movement for language renewal. Most teach the language of the tribe or tribes they serve. But classroom instruction is only one part of a much larger and more comprehensive effort to promote and rebuild these threatened languages. Across the United States, the tribal colleges have developed a comprehensive survival strategy that includes advocacy, research, curriculum development, and instruction.

To survive, a language must be respected. Tribal members must see its value and understand how it can strengthen and unite a community. Building this awareness is the first step in language renewal. And in more than two dozen reservations across the country, tribally controlled colleges are working consciously to build this necessary foundation of understanding.

Much of this work is informal, but it is never accidental. For example, many tribal colleges now use their language when naming campus buildings or identifying classrooms and offices. In addition, college leaders often make a point of speaking the tribal language in everyday conversation. On the Crow reservation, for example, LBHC president David Yarlott moves easily between English and Crow as he talks with faculty, staff, and students throughout the day. Leadership at the top helps establish both the legitimacy of the tribal language and its utility in everyday activities.

Many TCUs serve communities where languages are no longer widely spoken, which means that English must, for now, remain the language of college life. However, there is a growing movement to use the language to the greatest extent possible, especially in formal gatherings and community celebrations. For example, it is now typical for tribal college leaders to express greetings in their own language when speaking at public events. These introductory words serve an important symbolic role by uniting members, gathering the community together under the umbrella of culture, and presenting opportunities for public use of the language.

Increasingly, colleges are doing even more to elevate the value of their languages. At ANC, for example, students are now asked to introduce themselves in a tribal language when they rise to receive their graduation diplomas. In addition, college instructors are also encouraged to express greetings in a second language during new student orientations. Because most tribal college instructors are non-Indian, their willingness to speak the tribal language leaves an impression on students, according to President Carol Falcon-Chandler. "Students say, 'Gosh, if these instructors are speaking the language and they are not even from here, we'd better do it.'"

Several tribal colleges also manage public radio or television stations, which presents another opportunity to promote the language. On the Fort Belknap reservation, KGVA general manager Gerald Stiffarm blends English and Gros Ventre during his on-air interviews and encourages his young DJ's to both learn and use the language, even as they play a contemporary blend of Native American music, Top 40, and country tunes.

In addition, some colleges are also looking for ways to integrate language into all academic disciplines. At LBHC this effort is called "Crow across the curriculum" and it is reflected in efforts to link all instruction to the tribe's culture and language, according to President David Yarlott. For example, a computer course might require students to seek out an elder who can discuss the different parts of a computer in Crow.

A similar effort is underway at College of Menominee Nation, where the Menominee language is integrated into all courses to the greatest extent possible. According to Diana Morris, chief academic officer, this work not only supports the Menominee language, it also promotes greater academic achievement in all areas of study. Many students, for example, have difficulty in math and science, believing they are "non-Indian" disciplines that are not part of their heritage and irrelevant to their lives. Morris rejects this argument, pointing to the deep ecological knowledge and engineering achievements of Native societies in the past. By incorporating language and culture back into these courses, tribal colleges are "bringing [math and science] back into the community," she argued. "It's part of what we do."

At the heart of each tribal college's commitment to language survival is formal in-class instruction. Most TCUs offer one or two introductory level classes in the language of their tribe; some offer a great deal more. In communities where traditional languages have disappeared from daily use, this academic instruction often represents the only consistent effort to keep an endangered language alive.

The scope of this work is tremendous. Among the nation's 37 tribally controlled colleges dozens of languages are taught, from Diné and Lakota to Lummi and Blackfeet. Some languages, such as Ojibwe and Nakoda, are spoken by several tribes and offered at several colleges. Others, such as Tewa, are taught at only one college—and nowhere else in the world. It is a great and largely overlooked contribution to American scholarship. With little outside recognition or support tribal colleges are taking full responsibility for maintaining an important part of the nation's linguistic heritage.

The challenges are enormous. Because a growing number of students arrive with little or no exposure to their ancestral language, TCUs must start instruction at the introductory level, beginning with basic vocabulary and simple phrases. "I thought it would be easy to teach [Crow]," admitted Lark Real Bird, who is an instructor at LBHC, "but it's not." She assumed most students would have some familiarity with their own language. She was shocked to discover that most are now second language learners. Like all beginners, they face the challenge of mastering vocabulary, pronunciation, and grammar from scratch.

Language teachers know that one or two courses do not lead to fluency. Brief exposure over a handful of months is not, on its own, enough. However, they stress that fluency is not required to build a sense of pride and identity. To hear an ancestral language rise from silence—even when it is spoken hesitantly and imperfectly—is a magical experience. "I don't remember the [Aaniiih] language spoken in my lifetime," said Carole Falcon-Chandler. Now, however, she and ANC students have learned enough to greet each other in Aaniiih or Nakoda. Even a few words, some report, are enough to bring tears to the eyes of a grandmother who has not heard her language spoken since her childhood.

On the other hand, language faculty are eager to build on their successes and raise expectations. While few people believe tribal languages should replace English and most tribal college leaders do not anticipate the return of fully bilingual communities in the near future, greater fluency is the universal goal. At ANC, for example, one semester of language study is currently required for graduation and courses are available up to the intermediate level. But as their early efforts take root, there is talk of expanding the curriculum and raising requirements. American Indian Studies Director Sean Chandler is hoping to expand the number of language courses offered and add a second semester of language as a graduation requirement for those pursuing an associate degree.

On the Crow reservation, meanwhile, most of LBHC's language teachers feel that fluency must remain the focus of their work. Here, a sizable percentage of the population still speaks Crow and universal fluency is a recent memory. While rapid loss of the language caught many tribal members by surprise, they are unwilling to cede any ground: What was lost must be restored as quickly as possible. Here, all students pursuing an associate's degree are required to complete two semesters of Crow and two additional courses—Conversational Crow and Plains Indian Sign Language—are offered as electives.

Possibly the most comprehensive language curriculum exists at Diné College, which serves the sprawling Navajo Nation. Here, the Navajo language is still widely spoken and tribal culture is strongly felt. While the Navajo are also worried about the decline of language fluency, the relative strength of the language allows Diné College to offer a remarkably rich array of language courses. Some focus on the needs of second language learners, including a four-course sequence in Navajo as a second language, which moves students from the beginner to the advanced intermediate level. Other courses address the needs of students who already have conversational fluency, such as Navajo Literacy and Grammar for Speakers. There are also several specialized language courses, including Medical Terminology of the Navajo, Navajo Transcription, and Navajo Linguistics.

Many other tribal colleges are also making language instruction a special priority. Oglala Lakota College offers four levels of Lakota language instruction, from beginner to advanced. The highest, Lakota Language IV, requires students to write a research paper in the Lakota. Courses are also offered in Lakota grammar and public speaking. At Blackfeet Community College, it is possible to not only study Blackfeet, but to also earn an associate's degree in the language. Instruction is offered from the beginner to advanced levels. Several other TCUs serve two or more tribal groups and, therefore, teach multiple languages. For example, Salish Kootenai College on the Flathead Indian Reservation in western Montana teaches both Salish I and II, as well as Kootenai I and II.

It's important to stress that all TCUs are small institutions. Many of the colleges featured here maintain enrollments of between 250 and 500 students. The commitment to language instruction is, therefore, disproportionately large relative to enrollments and available resources. Even a limited number of course represents a deep commitment to language and culture.

Faculty who teach Spanish, French, or any other foreign language commonly offered in mainstream colleges have access to a wide array of textbooks and learning materials, from audiotapes to vocabulary flash cards. Students who want to study on their own, meanwhile, can purchase products ranging from Berlitz phrasebooks to complete Rosetta Stone courses. In contrast, tribal languages often have little or no instructional material. Indeed, some languages do not yet have their own comprehensive dictionaries. Language experts also note that existing materials are not always complete or reliable. Dictionaries compiled by missionaries, government agents, and other self-taught scholars in the 19th century might be only a few pages long, or reflect certain priorities (Bible translation) or discredited pet theories (that American Indians are a "lost tribe of Israel").

In this setting, tribes have two urgent tasks. First, they must work to document the language—its vocabulary and grammar—as quickly as possible in order to preserve the language in a form that will assure its survival even as the number of fluent speakers declines. Second, this work of documentation must be turned into instructional material appropriate for beginning language learners and then taught in a supportive and non-threatening environment.

Increasingly, tribes are taking greater responsibility for completing their own research—and much of this work is conducted by tribal college faculty. In the 1990s, for example, Albert White Hat Sr., a long-time language and culture instructor at Sinte Gleska University on the Rosebud reservation of South Dakota, compiled a comprehensive dictionary of the Lakota language and in 1999 authored *Reading and Writing the Lakota Language*, the first Lakota grammar ever developed by a tribal member. Appropriately, While Hat's work integrates cultural concepts into his text and emphasizes the role of language in tribal self-determination.[1]

More recently, Dr. Lanny Real Bird, who teaches Crow language at LBHC, compiled and continues to update a comprehensive Crow language dictionary. Drawing together preliminary work completed by missionaries and amateur scholars as well as his own extensive research, the thick text is by far the largest effort to date and it is used as the standard reference in the college's language courses.

---

[1] See Antoine, "Lakota Documentaries: Working with Cultural Heritage at a Tribal University," pp. 141-145.

In other cases, tribes are reaching out to professional linguists for assistance. ANC, for example, is working with University of Colorado linguist Allan Taylor, who first conducted some preliminary research on the Aaniiih language in the 1960s and then at the tribe's request compiled a dictionary in the 1980s. More recently, the tribal college asked Taylor to develop a complementary guide to Aaniiih grammar. Positive collaborations of this sort provide scholars with opportunities for research and practical resources for the tribal colleges.

Increasingly, TCU instructors are taking the next step by creating additional learning materials—textbooks, CD's, DVD's, flashcards, and more—that enrich classroom instruction. Few work with more energy and determination than Dr. Lanny Real Bird. Aside from compiling a Crow language dictionary, he devised a complete audio course in Plains sign language, supplemented with stacks of flash cards. He also developed an audio course in conversational Crow, which allows students to study on their own. Self-study material is urgently needed, he explained, because college courses are too short to teach fluency. He has even started developing materials for other tribal languages, including Dakota.

Real Bird accepts funding when it is available, but works—often at personal expense—even when it is not. And the results of this sustained effort now fill his office shelves. Stacked in one corner are cellophane-wrapped vocabulary flash cards and conversational DVD's that look as professional as anything made by a major publishing company. Video equipment fills the office and a machine capable of burning 10 DVD's at a time occupies much of his desk. Nearly single handed, he has created a comprehensive program of language instruction.

Similar efforts are taking place at tribal colleges across the country. In Barrow, Alaska, for example, Dr. Edna MacLean, former president of Iḷisaġvik College—the state's only TCU—recently completed recording the dialogue for a complete Rosetta Stone course in her increasingly endangered language. In addition to courses taught by the college, students and others can practice the language online. Many other instructors are quietly working to develop material for the classes they teach.

But teaching is not enough. Tribal college leaders must also help students overcome a reluctance to use the language in the community. In small and factionalized communities, language can be a source of friction and criticism. Arguments over pronunciation, writing systems, or use of borrowed words might reflect larger social tensions or frustration by some members that the language is changing. Young adults are sometimes told by fluent elders, "you're not saying it right," explains LBHC liberal arts instructor Tim **McCleary**, although this usually means that the young person is simply speaking with an accent. Even a few words of criticism might be enough to short circuit interest in learning the language.

In response, experienced tribal college instructors must work hard to create supportive and validating classroom experiences. "It's like 'What happens in Vegas, stays in Vegas,'" explained one teacher. Students must be allowed to make mistakes in class without fearing laughter or criticism. "We try to insulate our students from elders" during the first year of study, another said candidly. Empathy and gentleness is essential—along with a positive, can-do attitude. At Chief Dull Knife College, it is taboo to say that language learning is hard.

Support and encouragement is essential because instruction is pointless if students lack the confidence needed to speak the language in public. Tribal leaders often explain that between speakers and non-speakers, there is a frustratingly large third category of people: tribal members who simply refuse to speak their language. This group includes all ages and skill levels—and the usual explanation is that they fear making mistakes.

For language advocates, this self censorship is deeply frustrating. While tribal members debate writing systems and critique each other's pronunciation, the language is dying, argues CDKC President Richard Little Bear. He admonishes his students: "Speak! Speak to a telephone pole if you have to, but speak!" Fellow language instructor Burt Medicine Bull has another strategy. He provides his students with a ready reply when elders challenge their grammar or pronunciation: They should simply say, "Thank you for teaching me." Be respectful and treat every interaction as a learning opportunity, he advises, but have confidence in your own skills.

The best time to learn a second language is during childhood, according to linguists. Adults can learn, of course, but young children are already primed for language acquisition. They also have the time needed to build language skills and they can practice without the worries and angst experienced by some adult learners.

In response, a growing number of TCUs are investing time and resources needed to bring language programs to young tribal members. Some support summer language and culture camps where intensive interaction with the language is encouraged. While exposure to the language is limited to a few days or a few weeks, it's an opportunity to reach out to children and families in a festive way, say organizers.

In recent years, programs have been offered or sponsored by a wide range of colleges. CDKC, **Fond du Lac Tribal and Community College in Cloquet, Minnesota, and Bay Mills Community College in Brimley, Michigan, have all sponsored language immersion camp.** Others offer programs for preschool children. The latest initiative at CDKC is a language immersion daycare program. First offered in 2012 and funded by an Administration for Native Americans grant under the U.S. Health and Human Services Department, the program builds on its existing daycare program by incorporating formal instruction in Northern Cheyenne through games, songs, and other creative activities. Recognizing that parent involvement is an essential part of any early education program, the program also requires parents to attend several hours of language instruction several times a week. College leaders hope children and parents will continue to speak to each other in Northern Cheyenne.

The newest and most ambitious effort includes the founding of language immersion elementary schools where all subjects are taught and the Native language is used throughout the curriculum. These programs, while costly, offer the best hope of bringing languages back into daily use and, for this reason, generate a great deal of interest in Native communities across the country. Some work closely with tribal colleges and one school, White Clay Immersion School is both founded and supported by the tribal college, ANC. The school recently graduated its first eighth grade class and has helped bring the Aaniiih language back from the brink of extinction.[2]

White Clay Immersion School

The sunny classroom of the White Clay Immersion School is immediately familiar to anyone who recalls first grade. Child-sized desks face a whiteboard; posters, books and a colorful assortment of school supplies line the walls. Its only distinctive feature is the small class size—about a half dozen students are present—and the easy informality this intimate setting allows.

But as soon as their teacher begins to ask questions and the students offer their answers, it's clear that something unusual is taking place. Sprinkled amid the English is a liberal use of words and phrases from the Aaniiih language. While the school teaches all of the various subjects conventionally taught in elementary school, Aaniiih is—to the greatest extent possible—the language of instruction and informal conversation.

The White Clay Immersion School is one of a small but growing number of language immersion schools working to promote and sustain endangered tribal languages in the United States. Some are administered by tribes while others were founded as alternative charter schools. The White Clay School is the first and, so far, only immersion school founded and supported by a tribal college. Located on the campus of Aaniiih Nakoda College, it has its own building and enrolls 18 students in grades one through eight.

Immersion schools play an important role in language survival, according to Native educators, because they accomplish what most adult education language programs cannot: true language fluency. College courses can introduce a language but most adults stop learning before they achieve mastery. In contrast, immersion school students have the luxury

---

[2] See Umbhau, "Firing Up White Clay: Immersion School Students Encouraged to Return, Give Back," pp. 127-130; and Paskus, "More Than Words, A Way of Life: Language Restoration Programs Reach Beyond Tribal Colleges and Universities," pp. 38-46.

of time. At the White Clay Immersion School, students spend eight years interacting with the language—using it every school day and in nearly every class.

And the results are easily seen. While first and second graders gain familiarity with many words and phrases, much of their instruction must still take place in English. However, by the time students reach seventh and eighth grades, skills have deepened and even complicated writing assignments can be completed in the tribal language. On a recent spring day, for example, several eighth graders were polishing page-long graduation speeches—written entirely in Aaniiih.

Although the school's enrollment is small, the impact of its work is dramatic. According to Sean Chandler, a language instructor and director of American Indian Studies at ANC, only twelve elders still spoke the language when the school started in 2001. Today, only two elders remain. However, the school graduated its first cohort of four eighth graders in 2011 and continues to see enrollment growth every year.

"We were at a critical time," recalled school director Lynette Chandler. The language, she said, "was on the brink—I don't like to say extinction, but it was a very dangerous situation because of our [low] numbers." With a total enrollment of 18 students, every graduating class dramatically increases the number of fluent Aaniiih speakers.

Students benefit as well. They are offered a strong, academically focused curriculum and Lynette Chandler is told by high school teachers that her students do especially well in English and writing courses, confirming that a strong focus on second language proficiency builds skills in both languages. Equally important is the respect students receive in the community. As speakers of the Aaniiih language, the students are often asked to pray at community celebrations and other formal occasions. This nurtures a sense of purpose and pride that, according to many community leaders, is too often lacking from the lives of young tribal members.

Outcomes

Traditional languages have been under sustained attack for over 500 years. By the late 19th century, not a single tribe in the lower 48 states was untouched by aggressive governmental and missionary efforts to crush traditional languages and impose

English. In contrast, efforts to promote the survival of these languages are less than 50 years old and, in many communities, the work is just now beginning. But there is strong evidence that these early efforts are already making a difference.

Success is reflected first, and most tangibly, in the number of tribal members who are learning their ancestral languages. Most tribal colleges offer language courses and many require at least one semester of study as a graduation requirement for two or four year degrees. This is probably the largest sustained commitment to Native language instruction in the United States. Languages that have not been heard for a generation or more in some cases are now living inside classrooms and simple phrases are finding their way into communities.

While these required courses do not lead to fluency in most cases, it's important to emphasize that languages have value even when fluency is not achieved. In tribal communities all across the country, a sense of pride and social renewal is felt through even limited interaction with a language. An opportunity to greet an elder in a tribal language, discover a deeper understanding of culture through study of vocabulary and grammar, or feel the power of a prayer spoken in the original tongue produces the bonding and identity fundamental to personal pride and social cohesion.

But what is especially remarkable is the emergence of programs that actually do train fluent language speakers. Some colleges have the resources to teach courses to the advanced level and the founding of language immersion schools is accomplishing what skeptics long said was impossible: bringing lost or severely threatened languages back into the daily life of tribal communities. These programs offer hope and inspiration for Native communities across the country and around the world.

There is also a growing body of scholarship. It is remarkable that, despite a century or more of work by both amateur and professional linguists, so many tribal languages are insufficiently documented. TCU faculty, often working in collaboration professional linguists, are helping to fill the gaps by writing dictionaries, documenting grammars, and recording surviving speakers so that the languages can be preserved and taught. Equally important is the almost entirely neglected task of creating instructional material. In some communities, tribal colleges are the only institutions working to develop high quality programs of instruction.

Collectively, many tribal leaders view this work as an integral part of their mission to sustain cultural identities and address pressing social and economic ills. Sustaining and revitalizing languages is an essential step toward restoration of tribes as strong and healthy nations.

Next Steps and Needs

Language experts frequently note the lack of financial support for Indigenous language renewal. A variety of important federal and private sector initiatives do fund language restoration efforts. However, this support is dwarfed by the scope of the problem. In contrast to other academic areas such as math and science education, federal and private sector support for the study and promotion of tribal languages is miserly. Current funding cannot adequately serve the needs of all Native communities in the United States.

Tribal colleges have already accomplished a great deal with limited funding. Even modest increases in support will allow them to do even more. Looking to the future, for example, TCU faculty and administrators say they would like to expand current course offerings and to do even more in the areas of research and curriculum development. Even relatively small grants will accomplish a great deal in these areas.

More ambitiously, many tribal college leaders would like to expand their efforts to support language survival and instruction within the larger tribal community. Language camps, adult education programs, and immersion schools have a demonstrated track record of success, but are relatively expensive to develop and maintain. Yet without these efforts languages will remain threatened and many will continue to die. TCUs have the skills and credibility needed to nurture these programs, but often lack the necessary funding.

In the past, tribal colleges have benefited from outside support as they worked to develop strong and highly successful programs in a wide range of academic areas. They are successfully training teachers, nurses, computer engineers, biologists, artists, and other professionals who use their training to build stronger tribal communities. Many of these programs were nurtured in their early years by federal funds and private sector grants. At this moment of crisis, TCUs are turning their attention to the plight of their own languages. With support, they can help save and sustain this vital part of their—and America's—identity.

Paul Boyer, PhD, is the founding editor of Tribal College Journal *and author of* Capturing Education: Envisioning and Building the First Tribal Colleges.

Reference

De Lange, C. (2012). My Two Minds. *New Scientist, 2863,* 31–33.

More than Words, a Way of Life
Language Restoration Programs Reach Beyond Tribal Colleges and Universities

By Laura Paskus

On February 14, students at the White Clay Language Immersion School visited the staff and faculty at Aaniiih Nakoda College (ANC). They passed out Valentine's Day cards, then headed down to the college's career fair. "They get involved in everything," remarked President Carole Falcon-Chandler (member of the Aaniiih and of Nakoda descent), who is proud of the students and the school.

Founded in 2003, the school's mission is to "maintain the cultural integrity of the White Clay (Aaniiih) and Nakoda (Assiniboine) tribes." The school currently offers K-8 students the chance to learn their native language, A'ani. Since it's an immersion school, students don't simply sit through language classes for 50 minutes each day. Rather, students learn about science, math, and history while hearing, speaking, and experiencing the A'ani language. Classes in A'ani aren't just another attempt to fill out the day; they're an integral part of the whole learning experience.

When the school was founded, only 5 to 10 fluent A'ani speakers remained—in the entire world. Now educating its second generation of cohorts, the school has already doubled the number of A'ani speakers.

ANC's White Clay Immersion School is widely praised as the tribal college movement's first immersion language school. And while most tribal colleges have Native language programs and courses, increasingly they are creating language programs that reach into daycares, pre-schools, elementary schools, and beyond. This is vitally important work. According to a 2004 report from the American Indian College Fund, a total of 155 Indigenous

"More than Words, a Way of Life: Language Restoration Program Reach Beyond Tribal Colleges and Universities" appeared in *Tribal College: Journal of American Indian Higher Education, 24*(4), in summer 2013.

languages are today spoken in North America. Of those, 135 are spoken only by elders.

Today, tribal colleges and universities are at the forefront of language preservation, among college-age students and youth. "Those of us who are activists in trying to save the language have a hard time getting this across, even to our own people: That a language that has been viable for hundreds of years, maybe even thousands of years, is going away," says Chief Dull Knife College president Richard Littlebear (Northern Cheyenne). "All the unique references, all the unique humor, all the worldviews that go along with that—that might act as a conscience for a country like the United States—are slowly dying out." Littlebear is a graceful force for change on the Northern Cheyenne Indian Reservation and across Indian Country. And anyone who has attended an American Indian Higher Education Consortium meeting is familiar with his words. With an easy smile and spirited good humor, Littlebear is often invited to say a prayer before meals or to commemorate the end of a meeting.

Cheyenne is Littlebear's first language, and even when he has lived off-reservation, he kept the language moving through his mind. He also learned to read and write Cheyenne. At language workshops, he encourages speakers and teachers to do the same. "You don't have to use reading and writing to teach—that should be done orally," he says, "but learn to read and write your language so you can write your lesson plans and curricula." He also encourages people to create a literature of their language. Littlebear is perpetually playing with words, figuring out their alternative meanings and derivations, translating, and deciphering word puzzles. He also writes short stories and poetry. "When you write something like poetry, it's revealing a part of yourself that maybe you don't want to reveal. So it's hard," he says, explaining that he was initially reluctant when people encouraged him to share his poetry: "One of the arguments I came across was, 'Do it for the kids, do it for the future generations. If you're really interested in saving languages, in perpetuating languages, you should have it written down.'"

Chief Dull Knife College in Lame Deer, Montana, offers Cheyenne language classes and oversees a program at the tribal housing authority for those who want to learn about Cheyenne culture and language. Through a U.S. Department of Health and Human Service's Administration for Native Americans (ANA) grant, Cheyenne is taught to infants and young toddlers at the tribal college's daycare center. That project had a rocky start, says Littlebear, because the tribal college lacked experience teaching such young students. It's running more smoothly now, he says, but any new programs will face challenges. Teacher training is critical: For instance, someone who is fluent in the language may not be a natural-born teacher.

Littlebear himself leads a language reading and writing class for teachers who are then tested. If the teachers pass the test—which is not a given—they are certified and licensed to teach Cheyenne language and culture. "It took me 11 years to work up the nerve to take my own test, and I passed it," he says, chuckling with a characteristic joke: "That was kind of a harrowing experience, actually."

Every Wednesday, Littlebear also attends Cheyenne Soup Day, where Cheyenne speakers gather to eat, laugh, and tell stories. "It's a joy to hear all that. But in the back of my head, I keep thinking, 'Will this still occur 10 years from now?'" According to a 2010 survey, only 19% of people living on the Northern Cheyenne reservation spoke the Native language—down from 29% in the late 1990s.

"Everything seems to center around money and funds and all that," he says, adding that while grants—including the ANA grants many tribal colleges receive—fund crucial work, relying solely on them has its drawbacks. "In order for sustainability to occur, we have to do it on our own," he says. "The commitment has to come from the people, and we need to quit relying on government funds—they're too sporadic and too report-driven."

The real indication of success, says Littlebear, is making a fluent speaker of someone who had no experience whatsoever with the language. "Even here on the Northern Cheyenne reservation, I don't think we have produced a pure Cheyenne speaker. Maybe that's not possible anymore in this day and age, but that would be a good indicator," he says. Littlebear has seen changes at the tribal college, however: Cheyenne greetings ring up and down the hallways; students introduce themselves in their native language. "There's a new awareness of the language among the younger people, and they're really interested in it," he says. "Somehow, we have to keep going because they're only here for two years and then they're out. If we can keep lighting that spark, it might help."

In fact, many tribal colleges and universities are lighting that spark and prioritizing language programs. In 2008, the College of Menominee Nation's education program began training, certifying, and recertifying teachers—and helping them to integrate the Menominee language and culture into classroom curricula. And thanks to a grant from the U.S. Department of Health and Human Service's Administration for Native Americans, Stone Child College on the Rocky Boy's reservation has created the Cree Language Nest Planning Project and Cree language curriculum. The project's first phase includes a language immersion classroom for newborns and toddlers; the second phase will include a language nest classroom, where daycare and Cree immersion are combined.

At Sitting Bull College on the Standing Rock reservation in North Dakota, the Lakota Language Nest—*Lakȟól'iyapi Wahóȟpi*—is in its first year. In that immersion preschool, where children learn Lakota, instructors follow a curriculum based on one designed by the Maori people in New Zealand. In the "language nest" model, instructors focus on connecting children with elders, and help parents learn the language, too. The need for innovative language programs is crucial; today, there are only about 200 fluent Lakota speakers on the Standing Rock reservation.

Language restoration has long been a priority for Oglala Lakota College (OLC) president Thomas Shortbull. The tribal college, which serves the Pine Ridge reservation in South Dakota, offers a 12-hour immersion course for those seeking to learn the Lakota language. OLC also administers *Lakota Woglake*

Wounspe, a language immersion school in Porcupine, South Dakota, for K-4 students. According to Tom Raymond (Sicangu Lakota), OLC's dean of education and principal of Lakota Woglake Wounspe, between 25 and 30 students are currently enrolled at the school. Thanks to vehicles provided by OLC, they arrive from as far away as Pine Ridge and Kyle, each about 45 miles from Porcupine. Raymond says the school could serve even more children if it had more transportation options; he also hopes that the school can be expanded to someday extend through the fifth, eighth, or even twelfth grades.

At Lakota Woglake Wounspe, 99.9% of the instruction takes place in Lakota, says Raymond. There are four teachers, a school coordinator, two cooks, and a Council of Elders that offers its advice. "To truly understand this project, you have to rethink school and rethink how we learn language: [The students] are learning the language because they're learning how to *use* the language," he says. "Our students are learning math and language and science and social studies and all that—they are learning it through the use of the Lakota language."

To survive, says Raymond—who says he is not fluent in Lakota—a language must be used. It must be spoken, lived. "We tend to think of language as something to be used to communicate with people. The problem with that is the Lakota language is a way of life. It's part of a whole culture. You don't just learn a language, you learn a way of living," he says. "It reflects back on the old ways of life, when there was a lot of sharing, and traditional ways of living. I'm not talking about dancing back the buffalo, and everyone's wearing feathers and skins and lives in tipis. I'm talking about preserving a traditional way of life that is one with the world around." He adds that once a language has disappeared, it's not only the words that are gone—but also the culture, and a people. With Lakota Woglake Wounspe, OLC is trying to ensure that never happens to the Lakota language, or the Lakota people.

Meanwhile, far to the west and north, language programs are blooming across the North Slope—thanks to Iḷisaġvik College in Barrow, Alaska. The tribal college takes a multifaceted approach to teaching the Iñupiaq language, says Devin Bates, interim director of *Uqautchim Uglua*, the college's language program. Currently, only about 13% of Iñupiaq are fluent in their indigenous language.

Iḷisaġvik College offers classes in storytelling, conversation, grammar, and traditional dance. "In the traditional dance class every semester, students learn how to sing, how to drum, how to do the motion of the dances—and you can learn a lot of the language by repetition, by singing the songs, learning how to pronounce the words," says Mary Sage (Iñupiaq), Uqautchim Uglua's program coordinator. "We also have a carving class offered by a retired language teacher." He travels out to traditional villages across the North Slope, learning and teaching traditional carvings. There are also skin sewing classes, in which students learn to sew parkas, hats, boots, and mukluks. All of those classes solidify student connections to their native language.

Iḷisaġvik College also has its own immersion nest, which opened in November 2012, and serves preschool-aged students. Lessons and activities are conducted entirely in Iñupiaq, and students spend time with elders and attend field trips. In mid-February, for instance, students attended *Kivgiq*, or Messenger Feast, a massive cultural celebration held every few years in Barrow. The relative success of a program is hard to judge, especially when there are so few students. But, says Bates, those preschool students have started to speak Iñupiaq with their families and peers. "They're not fully fluent," he says, "but we're really seeing them move leaps and bounds forward."

The tribal college also works closely with other local institutions. The public school district, for instance, is developing a program—the Iñupiaq Learning Framework—to create curriculum standards for K-12 classrooms. It also devised a visual Iñupiaq vocabulary program, an online database, and has worked with the staff of the Rosetta Stone Endangered Language Program to develop a CD-ROM for Iñupiaq.

In partnership with the Barrow Office of the Mayor and the North Slope Borough Heritage Center, the tribal college also holds regular cultural events. Their first event, says Sage, was called *Uqapiaqta*—"Let's speak," or "Let's talk Iñupiaq." They coordinated with hunters who donated four seals. "We went to the heritage center's traditional room, where we could get messy, and butchered the four seals," she says. "We invited the community, and elders, and learned how to cut up the seals, to butcher, and also learned the names of the parts in the Iñupiaq language." Once a month, she says, they organize events centered on traditional skills and learning the Iñupiaq language. "You could see a lot of smiles," she says, "a lot of learning."

While much has changed in recent decades, North Slope communities still engage in many aspects of traditional cultural life. Whaling still occurs each spring and fall, says Sage. And there are traditional events, feasts, and dances, as well as gift-giving, bartering, and fun. "There are still a lot of things that we do, like hunting, skin sewing, dancing, camping," she says. "The only thing that's different is we're not fluent." Almost everyone under the age of 45, she says, is unable to speak Iñupiaq.

But that's changing. "There is the recognition that it's time to learn the language—and use the language before we no longer have it," says Sage. "My children say what they can. Their grandmother was their babysitter; they can understand the basics, and they love using Iñupiaq words." At home, her children use the online Iñupiaq language tools available to them. They get excited, she says, when they earn top grades on the program—and she can hear them shouting out, proud of themselves.

As for the college's program director, Devin Bates, he too is learning Iñupiaq—even though he is non-Native. "The ability to speak Iñupiaq goes beyond words," he says. "The Iñupiaq language is an expressive language; it's a very rich language, and it has single words that—in the way that they work and the things they express—rival or exceed English at a post-doctoral level." One of those words, he says, is *Ikiaqtalaaq,* which means, "to flame or tingle because of emotional status." Bates explains: "It means basically, that your whole soul is pregnant, that you're tingling inside. Just one word means all that! There are words for concepts that don't exist in English. You can't learn them and know them without living here, being here. And when that happens, it becomes transformative. It's very personal, very sacred."

Sage and Bates are both optimistic for the future of language programs at Iḷisaġvik College—and for the revitalization of the Iñupiaq language. "We're really shooting for language nest expansion across the North Slope. At this early stage and with the past history of language degradation and people being deported out to boarding schools, there are a lot of wounds that run really deep," says Bates. "But the community desperately wants this. Iñupiaq is very much alive—there just needs to be some catalyst, something that breaks the barriers that history and experience have put up."

In North America, and worldwide, Indigenous languages are disappearing at an alarming rate. But there are models of success for language revitalization. Richard Littlebear points to the current use of languages, such as Hebrew, Maori, or Hawaiian, that were once on the brink of disappearance. There is hope. And if Littlebear is a role model, the hard work of language revitalization can be accomplished with humor and joy.

Whether the language learners are tribal college students greeting one another in their native language, kindergarteners seated in a semi-circle around an elder, or people laughing and sharing a meal together, the joy of language learning segues into something serious. The language programs at tribal colleges and within Native communities across North America represent a way for young people to connect more deeply with the past—to understand and speak the words their ancestors uttered, call the features on their homelands by ancient names, and sing traditional prayers with confidence—and to stitch together the threads of a vibrant future for their tribes.

Laura Paskus is a former managing editor of Tribal College Journal.

VOICES

Over the past quarter century, thinking on language revitalization has evolved with one of the most important shifts being the general consensus that immersion is the best strategy for producing fluent speakers. But there has also been a remarkable degree of consistency over that time in the philosophies and perspectives on language revitalization. Although the timbre of the voices may differ, the authors of all of the articles reprinted here are in agreement on overarching tenants, strategies, and the significance of revitalizing Indigenous languages at tribal colleges and beyond.

In "Finding a Place for Navajo: English Must be Restricted if the Navajo Language is to Survive," published in 1993, Diné College instructor Clay Slate maintains that while English is useful, it should be constrained to "carefully chosen places." He argues for the creation of an "authoritative language planning agency," that develops strategies on strengthening the Indigenous language. Slate's article is focused on Diné and the Navajo Nation, but his analysis and arguments can be applied to all Native languages and nations. One of the highlights of this essay is Slate's reading of sociolinguist Joshua Fishman's eight stages in the life cycle of a language. The author applies this to Navajo and uses it to buttress his argument for restricting English.

Richard Littlebear, president of Chief Dull Knife College and one of the foremost thinkers on language revitalization, penned "To Save Our Languages, We Must Change Our Teaching Methods" in 2000, offering a look back at language revitalization philosophy at the turn of the millennium. An early advocate of immersion, Littlebear stresses that Native languages are oral traditions, not written ones, and that they should be taught as such. Everyday conversation is vital, he stresses, and fluency stems from speaking. Littlebear has always embraced linguistic innovation and has argued that the creation of new words is a sign of a living language. His analysis remains as salient today as it was then.

Tammy Eastman DeCoteau, who served as the field manager of the Association on American Indian Affairs' Midwest office, similarly stresses the importance of living Indigenous languages and raises serious concerns about their survival in her article, "Who Will Teach My Great-Great-Grandchildren Dakotah?" DeCoteau penned her essay in 2004, when she was a student at Sisseton Wahpeton College. Her language instructor there inspired her to write it and she went on to help raise $50,000 for language revitalization efforts at the college. Her article offers a student perspective and reveals some of the grave concerns that the younger generations have as the population of fluent speakers ages and passes on.

The same year that TCJ published DeCoteau's op-ed, Richard Littlebear penned his oft-cited article, "One Man, Two Languages: Confessions of a Freedom-Loving Bilingual." He takes aim at the English-only movement that spearheaded California's infamous Proposition 227, which sought to eliminate bilingual education. Although the bill's authors were primarily concerned with Spanish, Littlebear makes the logical connection that such legislation is a threat to Native languages. He points out that U.S. English Inc., English First, and other anti-bilingual organizations wrap themselves in the flag, but are in conflict with many of the United States' founding principles as articulated in the Constitution and Declaration of Independence.

The next two pieces are transcriptions of speeches given before the Senate Committee on Indian Affairs in 2014. The first, "'We Are Resilient, and We Are Succeeding,'" is the voice of Oglala Lakota College president Thomas Shortbull, who outlines Oglala Lakota College's language revitalization efforts, but notes the great financial struggle that both his college and all TCUs face. Shortbull stresses the importance of reauthorizing the Native American Programs Act of 1974 to Ensure the Survival and Vitality of Native Languages. "TCUs are holistic institutions and therefore language revitalization is essential to this," he states. Without steady funding, he argues, their education efforts are jeopardized.

Similarly, Clarena Brockie, the dean of students at Aaniiih Nakoda College and a former Montana state legislator, underscores the tremendous importance of federal support for language revitalization programming. She points out that prior to contact in 1492, hundreds of Native languages existed throughout North America. Since then, however, only 15 or 20 persist as living languages spoken by tribal members who are not elders. Brockie recounts how her Aaniiih language faced near extinction in 1997, when just 26 fluent elders remained. But with federal funding, the college was able to launch the White Clay Immersion School and revitalize the language. Despite Aaniiih's success, Brockie warns that the situation remains precarious: "Once a language becomes extinct it takes with it much of the history, philosophy, ceremonies, culture, and environmental and scientific knowledge of the people who spoke it."

The final article in this section, "Native Languages Preserve Our Way of Thinking and Knowing," comes from Richard B. Williams, the former CEO and president of the American Indian College Fund. During his tenure with the College Fund, Williams observed firsthand the powerful effect that language revitalization programs have on children and adults alike. He argues passionately that Western educational models have failed Native peoples and that there are myriad benefits to Indigenous language acquisition, including strengthening cultural connections, improving self-image, and enhancing cognitive development.

Finding a Place for Navajo
English Must Be Restricted if the Navajo Language Is to Survive

By Clay Slate

For describing the objects, interests, and values of the Navajo world, no other language than Navajo will ever be adequate. When we speak of the "culture" that Navajos love and revere, much of what we refer to is something built of the brick and mortar of language: songs, prayers, laws, tales, greetings, introductions, cures, blessings, directions, recipes, jokes, philosophy, history, teachings, and more.

The loss of Navajo, which is still spoken by at least 80,000 people, would mean, for the individual or the community, a destruction of intimacy, the dismemberment of family and community, the loss of a rooted identity. Maintaining the Navajo language through the generations can mend the Navajo social fabric and overcome the sociocultural dislocation so often seen in Navajo youth. Language is the rich and dynamic rallying point with which a society identifies itself.

No one should claim that those Navajos who do not speak Navajo are any less Navajo than the others. But being Navajo in Navajo is different from being Navajo in English, and a society that allows people to be Navajo in Navajo is worth maintaining. For whatever reasons, a Navajo who speaks only English is more likely to move away, more likely to marry someone of another ethnic group, more likely to change traditions. These are all practices that any Navajo has every right to pursue, but they do not promote cultural continuity. To preserve the language and culture of the Navajo, we must promote access to a rich life for those who would be Navajo in Navajo.

Today, Navajo society has two languages with strong standing, a situation which linguists refer to as diglossia. In 1930, this was not true—nearly all Navajos spoke only Navajo, although a few

"Finding a Place for Navajo: English Must Be Restricted if the Navajo Language is to Survive" appeared in *Tribal College: Journal of American Indian Higher Education, 4*(4), in spring 1993.

also spoke Spanish. But by the year 2130, without some successful social engineering, nearly all Navajos will be monolingual English speakers. Thus, we are watching a change in language use. This process is called a shifting diglossia.

Faced with this fact, the challenge is simple: We must stop the shift. But how do we attain a stable diglossia? Any attempt to rebuild a monolingual Navajo society would be futile and stupid; no one wants this. English is extremely useful, and it is good for Navajos to master. However, the work of linguists has shown that when English is allowed into every social space, it will eventually completely replace the traditional language.

A move to preserve a language is not a move "back to the blanket." It is instead a careful use of the treasure that a people has inherited as a people. The treasure is not hard and cold; it is alive and organic, and must be fed and nurtured. This process requires for a society a measured amount of turning inward, to speak with those who speak the language, so that the continuity between generations is not broken.

The need then is to ensure that some carefully chosen places (as well as topics, functions, events and relationships) rigorously exclude English. The exclusive use of Navajo must be secure and normal in those spaces before the diglossia will be stable and before the bilingualism of our society will stop shifting. Otherwise, Navajo will eventually be silent.

But how does one choose these social spaces? What kinds of talk should be reserved for Navajo? Where should it take place, and with whom, and for what purposes?

The work of Joshua Fishman, a founder of sociolinguistics, provides some useful clues. In his book, *Reversing Language Shift*, he examines about a dozen different attempts to preserve endangered languages around the world. Among the many sad stories of language loss (there are hundreds; he describes a half dozen carefully), there are a few success stories (he mentions several, and describes three carefully).

In his analysis of both types of struggle, he shows us eight stages of strength and security that a language goes through. Stage one classifies a language that is at its strongest possible position; stage eight is that of a language very close to language death.

To begin, it is helpful to understand Fishman's eight stages and examine Navajo in these terms. However, this is not meant to be a cookbook. I hope that it is one voice among many in a thorough and thoughtful dialogue.

Stage 8

Here a language is at its weakest. A language at stage eight has only a few older people who still speak the language, and they are isolated from one another. This does not apply to Navajo in any communities on or near the Navajo Nation.

Stage 7

Here a language has a number of middle-aged and older speakers who speak the language regularly to one another, but they are all beyond child-bearing age, and have not taught the language to their children. Some Navajo communities and families, particularly in the border towns and larger on-reservation communities, are now approaching this serious condition. Even if these older people come together for lots of talk, events, and social gatherings in Navajo, the language will not last at this stage. No more young speakers will be coming along. The family can make all the "visits to grandma" that they want; in very few cases will that have any lasting effect.

Stage 6

This is the key stage. It is on the defense of this stage that most efforts should focus. Here the language is still used in the home, from parents to children. The home is still insulated by a family, a neighborhood, and a community that speaks Navajo. This world of home/family/neighborhood/community is usually the whole of a child's world, who, if raised here, in Navajo, will have Navajo as the language of the heart for her or his whole life. If children do not learn the language in the home, all other efforts must be repeated every generation, until society tires of paying for them.

Efforts to find a stable diglossia must focus upon making stage six a healthy and protected place for Navajo. Other uses of limited resources are just Band-Aids and of small importance in the struggle to perpetuate Navajo. For example, at Navajo Community College 14 different postsecondary Navajo language courses are taught to almost 500 students per semester. However, very little of what we do will have any effect at all on whether parents speak Navajo to their children in the home. I point this out not to denigrate our efforts at the college, but to make completely clear that even the best intentioned and most interesting efforts may have little direct effect on language survival.

The strength and connectedness of a community becomes important when trying to protect stage six. Certainly the housing patterns that we see in new construction around the Navajo Nation do not always result in a community, nor do the school and other compounds. The solution may be found in discussions at community events such as at church gatherings, graduation dinners, and NAC meetings, and may focus on the issues of clan and family.

The important factor is this, however: one family, or two or three isolated homes dedicated to Navajo, is not enough. At the least, a true community of Navajo speakers, with families having three generations of speakers, must gather consciously as insulation for those who raise their children in Navajo. This is the necessary minimum.

Stage 5

Languages here have local literacy in the community, neighborhood, family and home. Navajo has very little of this now, although the renewed interest in Navajo literacy makes this possible for the future. There is some Navajo literacy in the churches, and some Navajo reading material is available, but as yet no vibrant Navajo reading and writing exists to help feed stage six.

Stage 4

This is where the language is in the schools. Most of the schools at this point that have Navajo have it only in a token way (usually only to support English instruction), treating the language as only a secondary and passing concern. The institutional context is such that Navajo is subtly but powerfully unwelcome.

For instance, in a school where a friend of mine teaches, the majority of the children at least understand Navajo, yet she never hears it in the halls. When Navajo is taught in schools, there is often no distinction drawn between teaching Navajo to speakers and teaching it to non-speakers, with the result that all students are in one unmanageable class, which is frustrating for both groups.

A few schools do more. The only schools that can affect the survival of Navajo positively are those which openly and completely stand for the language and culture of Navajo. At a few of these schools (including Navajo Community College) even some of the instruction in content areas is done in Navajo. Navajo language work in these schools is effective when it is understood how the language is used outside of the school, and instruction emphasizes expansion of students' skills for using that Navajo.

Like all school subjects, language learned in school fades rapidly when not exercised. Since the funding, and thus the real control, of Navajo schools comes from the outside, there is little committed Navajo work done in most schools, although exceptions do exist. Even in schools most committed to Navajo, English is still the language of power, with an underlying message that English provides the route to success. Although the Navajo Nation education policies of 1984 take a strong pro-Navajo position, there has been only sporadic and minimal follow-through.

It is most important to remember what the schools can and cannot do. Any school effort that does not directly affect the home/family/neighborhood/community dynamic is probably not central to the language survival question. To this extent, those who have fought against having Navajo in the schools by saying that it should be taught only in the home (with only English in the schools) have been half right. If we expect the schools to perpetuate Navajo, we will be ultimately disappointed. In general, they will provide too little, too late.

Stage 3

Here the endangered language is used in the lower work sphere away from the community between Navajos, and is used by government and business for some Navajo customers or clients. Although Navajo still has activity at stage three, there are certainly many public places away from the community where Navajo is spoken only quietly, if at all, and the social stigmas attached to the use of Navajo are strong.

Examples of this abound: at one of the large mines, Navajo is prohibited on the walkie-talkies on the specious grounds that if there is an emergency it is important that everyone understand.

Stage 2

Here the language is used in the upper work sphere and in the media. Navajo is occasionally present here, as on the Navajo Nation 50,000-watt AM station KTNN, and other radio stations, but there is little Navajo television and no regular Navajo in any newspaper. Again, however, if there are to be efforts in this area, they will only be symbolic, and perhaps wasteful, if they are not planned in such a way as to impact stage six.

Stage 1

Here the language is being used at the highest levels of government, work, media, and education. Again, Navajo is occasionally present at this level (e.g., in Navajo Nation Council deliberations), but only sporadically, and English seems to be driving it out. Official policy moves to exclude all languages but English from parts of stages one and two that threaten Navajo.

***

The centerpiece of this analytical scheme is that all effective activities geared to preserve the Navajo language must ultimately focus on secure and protected use of Navajo in the home/family/neighborhood/community. Any other efforts are just "blowing air into a flat tire." Although this focus on the protected home environment may seem clear, it is a difficult task to influence daily informal life, and only communities of speakers who are committed to this goal can succeed.

Still, the focus must remain at this local level, for it is the language of the home that is infused with emotion, identity and intimacy. It is the "language of the ordinary, informal, spontaneous, and affectionate heart," writes Fishman, and it is only here that the language will be fully exercised in the culture.

Thus, we must get official Navajo Nation recognition that rural Navajo communities in which the language is still rich and protected are treasure-houses for the Navajo Nation, and must be supported as such. It is here that the Navajo language builds community and community builds language.

At other places where Navajo is no longer the normal or only language of the community—such as Kayenta, Window Rock, and the border towns—a different effort toward revitalizing community through revitalizing language is called for. Each community should plan and carry out its own Navajo language-enriching activities (drama, readings, lectures, music, culture, traditional arts, etc.), with input from every portion of the community.

At the Navajo Nation level, there is a need for an authoritative language planning agency (a new office has recently been opened at the Navajo Division of Education that may take on the duties of nationwide language preservation). Such an agency would develop a strategy for language work at the home/ family/ neighborhood/ community level. It would focus that strategy on specific projects at specific places and carry out and monitor those activities.

All activities would be measured against the standard of whether or not they impacted stage six. For example, if the Navajo language school work was well-integrated so the content of the lessons matched the vocabulary and functions of home use of Navajo, it would be most effective.

Care must be taken not to rush too quickly into activities at stages one through five, if stage six had not yet been addressed. It is easy to feel good about nice public performances in Navajo, or about fancy dictionary projects or computer programs. But their value is diminished when the essential work has not been addressed.

Certainly for those communities where stage six is still healthy, it is useful to address stages one to five, in order to provide further insulation and security for Navajo in the home. But for those communities that are closer to stage seven, with the only viable community being speakers beyond child-bearing age, the most important task would be to rebuild stage six, and provide family, neighborhood and community support for those parents who are speaking Navajo to their children in the home. Any other activities miss the center of the target.

Knowing when to move beyond a focus on stage six and to concentrate on strengthening the language in broader contexts is not an exact science. These questions must be constantly examined by expert Navajo practitioners in the field, people who are actively working to preserve the language. Beyond stage six work, it can be important to enrich the language through expansion of the Navajo vocabulary and to develop adults' language skills.

For example, local media can be encouraged to have regular Navajo language offerings for their audience. Further, there are stage four activities, such as Navajo immersion Head Start centers, that could be very powerful if they are preceded and followed by life-long activity in Navajo for the children.

As a central issue, we ask: what kinds of talk are most important to protect? Where will English be completely excluded, and with which topics, in which relationships, and for what purposes? In answering these questions, we will discover the shape of the Navajo speaking community, in all of its complexity and learn why some settings seem to welcome Navajo, and others press it down. We must decide which highly critical functions to protect, and with which populations.

Specific steps must be taken, and on specific timelines. However, there is room for more than one sort of Navajo-speaking community. For example, some Navajo speakers practice the traditional ways, and some do not. This is normal; the language can encompass both. But all will be actively expressing Navajo identity through the Navajo language.

Preservation of Navajo is enhanced by the fact that the Navajo people have their own land. Yet this alone will not be enough. Within that land, there must now be formed concentrations of those who will actively protect the language. The choice of exactly what to protect must be made according to two principles. First, do that which will most clearly aid parents in using Navajo with their children, and, second, choose what can practically be done.

As an example, I will suggest one type of talk, the social introduction, that should be seriously considered for establishment as a Navajo-only social space. A traditional Navajo introduction, through which two people come to be acquainted, is a clearly defined and circumscribed piece of talk. It involves, at the minimum, giving one's clan information, telling where one is from, and establishing a traditional way to address the new acquaintance.

For those who speak Navajo fluently and articulately, a great deal more can be said, often resulting in the establishment of an understanding of (perhaps distant) blood relationship. But even for those Navajos who have little command of the language, a formulaic recital of clan information, and a sufficient understanding of clan structure to arrive at appropriate terms of address, can be mastered in a fairly short time.

For strengthening the home/ family/ neighborhood/ community nexus of Navajo, the terms used are exactly the personal referents of the home and family, and the information exchanged can deeply affect even one's very future. For example, the Navajo Nation council recently passed a law, consonant with traditional practice, prohibiting marriage within one's own clan.

If all or many Navajos were to exclude English from this social space, a powerful tool for mending the fabric of Navajo society would be unleashed, a tool that could bring homes, families, neighborhoods, communities, clans, even the entire Navajo Nation, closer together in a bond of being Navajo through the Navajo language. This kind of talk is but one example, and possibly not even the right one. The menu is full of possibilities.

Each decision about what to do will be colored by an important principle: to maintain the viability of Navajo, there is a need to maintain cultural boundaries, a need for an intermittent detachment from the mainstream of Western society, a time that Navajos would turn only to Navajos, in Navajo. To center the effort at the home/family/neighborhood/community nexus focuses on having the language taught by parents, to children, and concentrates on the non-power, private sphere.

English is still promoted, but in its own place, and if it is rigorously excluded from the Navajo social spaces, the wholeness of a Navajo society nurturing itself in Navajo can be kept.

There will be a paranoid criticism from Anglos calling this effort insubordinate, economically backward, and an insult to the public order. There will be resistance from Navajos who do not speak Navajo or who will not admit to speaking it, and those who are fashioning a new identity and are caught in the middle.

These people, of course, are no less Navajo than those who choose to be Navajo through the Navajo language. The move to preserve Navajo should not become a new cultural chauvinism, denigrating those who do not learn Navajo; their path is only a different path, and both are valid.

The challenge is how to use the immense resources still at our disposal—especially the tens of thousands of fluent and articulate speakers—to protect the cultural boundaries of stage six, and to send a message that competence in Navajo is a young person's birthright and responsibility. The struggle, if it is to be fought out, will be immensely difficult. Do not discount the pessimists and alarmists who predict and announce losses. Eternal watchfulness will be the price of maintaining Navajo. But if this cannot be done for Navajo, perhaps it cannot be done for any Native American language.

Clay Slate directed Navajo Community College's Navajo Language Program.

Reference

Fishman, J.A. (1991). *Reversing Language Shift: Theoretical and Empirical Foundations of Assistance to Threatened Languages.* England: Clevedon.

To Save Our Languages, We Must Change Our Teaching Methods

By Richard Littlebear

The speakers of American Indian languages are breaking camp and journeying on to camps in the spirit world. Unless we start saving our languages immediately, we will lose them. In my travels over the years to various language teaching programs in Alaska, Canada, and many of the contiguous 48 states, I have seen certain practices that make us unwitting accomplices in this loss.

Emphasizing Writing over Speaking

We learned to speak our languages from other speakers. If we made a mistake when we spoke, our elders would repeat the utterance, and we would catch on. Thus we acquired the smallest sounds of our languages. The simple act of speaking taught us to speak them correctly.

We seem to forget that we acquire fluency by speaking. That may sound trite, but in our language classes, we often emphasize writing over speaking. There is no clear understanding of first and second language acquisition principles. I think all teachers regardless of their specialties or endorsements should learn these principles, but that's another article.

Our languages must be taught orally. Many teachers assume that we must first write our languages in order to speak them. How did we come to this assumption? We had bad language teaching models. Most of our language teaching programs imitate the way English is taught—emphasizing grammar.

We all remember learning the tenses and parts of speech, conjugating verbs, and writing English, usually as punishment. Remember how tedious that was? Yet we persist in making our students do the same things in our own languages. Many language teachers teach writing even when that language has no writing system—and even when those teachers have minimal skills in

---

"To Save Our Languages, We Must Change Our Teaching Methods" appeared in *Tribal College: Journal of American Indian Higher Education, 11*(3), spring 2000.

writing in English or their own tribal languages. This is amazing for languages that were, up until very recently, primarily oral.

We should speak our languages or teach speaking to anyone who will listen. When taught that way, our languages are acquired in a natural context, which is essential for fluency and coherence.

Teaching Words Out of Context

Our languages must be taught in the context of every day conversation, not as isolated words. A person can say in English, "tie your shoes," and it is acceptable. In Cheyenne, we could also say that, but it would evoke a ridiculous image of someone taking a pair of shoes and literally tying two shoes into a knot. In Cheyenne the whole group of words changes; there is no reference to "tying" or to "shoes." The correct Cheyenne command simply means "lace your shoes." Similar linguistic phenomena occur in other American Indian languages.

By teaching isolated words, we are creating whole tribes that will speak only in numbers, or colors, or body parts with nothing linking them. Speakers will dutifully utter "nine," or "knee," or "red" whenever they receive the right stimuli. But numbers have to connect to something; something has to have color; body parts must have functions.

It is good to know the basic words, but these words often get modified or disappear entirely when used in the proper conversational environments. Let's teach our languages as they are spoken while we can.

Not Inventing New Words

"Ko'konôxo'êustonestôtsetseohketo'seto'taamenôtove-ohetanoto" could be the Cheyenne word for "computer." The word means "the tapping-writing object that almost knows how to think for itself." It "could be" the Cheyenne word for computer, but it will never be because our language has quit inventing and accepting new words that designate contemporary phenomena.

In an earlier time, despite its formidable length, this word would have been easily acquired and used orally by potential speakers of Cheyenne. That's because when it is taught orally, we have no idea of the length of this word. It's just a series of sounds, and therefore we cannot attribute degrees of difficulty to it.

Because we don't invent new Cheyenne words, our language is overwhelmed by each new object, term, or idea that appears on the contemporary scene. When we have no word, we just pucker our lips and point them towards the object we are talking about. Instead of puckering up our lips, we should make new words.

Changing Our Ways

Our tribes now have to use schools to teach and perpetuate our languages. Schools are hostile venues for languages, which were not meant to be taught that way. As we try to mold our languages to fit into schools, we must develop curricula, teaching methods, and assessment instruments that are acceptable to state standards, parents, teachers, and American Indian elders. We have never had to do these things before for our languages, but now we must. We have no choice because our families are no longer teaching the youth how to speak.

Our elders must help us save our languages instead of ridiculing their grandchildren and other potential speakers who happen to make a mistake in pronunciation. We should sensitize our elders to the damage of such ridicule.

We wrongly assumed our languages would live forever, but they are dying. Our language teaching programs cannot afford to fail. Our failures heap disrespect on our holy languages.

I believe that Cheyenne is sacred and holy and came from the Great Spirit. Did it come from *Ma'heo'o* as isolated words, in written form? Was it intended to be stagnant and never grow?

I think not. We are attempting to preserve our languages in a hostile environment, contemporary America. We must change many of our teaching practices if we are to succeed.

Richard Littlebear, EdD, is the president of Dull Knife College.

Who Will Teach My Great-Great-Grandchildren Dakotah?

By Tammy Eastman DeCoteau

Sometime in the distant future, I will have great-great-grandchildren, and I think about what their world will be like if the Dakotah language is dead. I am working hard to help revitalize the Dakotah language, but I also worry about what I am not accomplishing. There is no Dakotah word for how many times I have wanted to give up the effort.

Then, I speak with an elder, and I remember why giving up would dishonor those elders who struggled to save their language and culture when these things were outlawed in days past.

I recall a story about Vince Robertson who was beaten by a nun at a Catholic boarding school until his legs were black and he needed to go to the hospital—because he was caught speaking Dakotah.

I met a woman who learned Dakotah in college and through books. When she speaks, the words are the right words, but the way they are said is not right. Is that the way my great-great-grandchildren will speak, if they learn to speak Dakotah at all?

Maybe some future linguist will be paid a zillion dollars to bring back our language. And I wonder again how my great-great-grandchildren will speak Dakotah. For example, the word *maka* (dirt), the word *maka* (skunk), and the word *maġa* (goose) are pretty close to each other. You know which one it is by the way that the word comes out of your mouth. Will that future linguist teach my great-great-grandchildren how to go digging in a skunk?

Our fluent speakers are elders. If I want to know what *sotoju* means today, it is a simple phone call away or a trip to someone's house. But often the elders say, "I am forgetting, too, because I hardly speak it anymore."

It is getting harder all the time to find a place to listen to the language. There are two or three tribal elders who regularly go to

"Who Will Teach My Great-Great Grandchildren Dakotah?" appeared in *Tribal College: Journal of American Indian Higher Education, 15*(4), spring 2004

the Dakota Connection in the mornings because they have breakfast for $1.55 if you are 55 or older. I know that it is impolite, but I ask to sit with them just to listen. I try to go to the tribal elderly nutrition center for lunch once a week too, but lately, there has been no Dakotah spoken there. It is very sad.

Although many people sing Dakota hymns, I would guess that 99 out of 100 don't know what they are singing. Even some of our most wonderful singers mispronounce words. For example, the sound for *śa* is not the sound for *s'a*. They are very different and distinct sounds.

Grandparents no longer tell stories to their grandchildren. When people get home after a long day of work, and kids get home after a long day of school, they all vegetate in front of a television. So we depend on the schools to teach our children.

Nathan Thompson says, "Learning the Dakotah language is like building a tipi. You can't put up all the poles at once—it won't come out even. You have to put the poles up one by one—then it will be strong. That's how you learn the language. Take your time. Take your time."

Lucy Keeble said, "*Amapeb ġaś henuh dehan Dakod iwaye*," which means something like, "Even though they hit me, I still speak Dakota."

We are lucky. The Lake Traverse reservation where I live in South Dakota still has many speakers—elders who hold the future of our language in their hands. People say that you don't realize how valuable something is until you've lost it. We need to help our elders to pass it on, so that my great-great-grandchildren can learn Dakotah.

Tammy Eastman DeCoteau is the director of the Dakotah Language Institute.

One Man, Two Languages
Confessions of a Freedom-Loving Bilingual

By Richard Littlebear

When the movement for "English only" began some years ago, I told participants at a bilingual education workshop that I was against it. A teacher there asked me why. I was so shocked by her question that I had no ready answer, and my silence has bothered me ever since.

I was unable to answer because I had never thought that advocating speaking, reading, writing, and thinking only in English might eventually become such a divisive topic. I was rendered momentarily mute because I had thought that the English-only proponents could not curtail the freedom of expression guaranteed by the U.S. Constitution. With their red, white, and blue proclamations and websites, they try to make the speaking of only English into a near-patriotic event.

The way I understood them, the framers of the Constitution guaranteed freedom of expression; they did not qualify that freedom by saying it could be exercised only in English or only in some other language, for that matter.

I have often questioned the direction this country takes in regards to civil rights, human rights, and especially the freedom to express ourselves. The ideals propounded in the Declaration of Independence, the Constitution, and the Bill of Rights are excellent. This country's proactive striving towards those ideals is still the best effort by any government to reach those ideals. Although sometimes diverted by self-interest groups, this effort encourages members of a minority like me.

It keeps me hopeful in spite of the fact that the government of this country deliberately tried to annihilate my Cheyenne ancestors in the 19th century and tried to kill our language, culture, and spiritualism at the same time. Even now, at the dawn of the 21st century, these attacks still occur in both overt and covert forms.

"One Man, Two Languages: Confessions of a Freedom-Loving Bilingual" appeared in *Tribal College: Journal of American Indian Higher Education, 15*(4), in spring 2004.

My reaction to the teacher's question was primarily emotional; I feel the English-only movement is just another way of killing the Cheyenne language and other Native American languages. These English-only people have wholly missed the lesson of freedom—freedom for people like me even if I don't speak the Queen's English, even if I don't look like Thomas Jefferson or George W. Bush or Dolly Madison or Pat Nixon.

Essence of Our Being

I am a freedom-loving person who happens to think, speak, and write daily in two languages. I read the research, conveniently ignored by English-only advocates, which proves that bilingual education and immersion in Native language classes work; these Native students do better on standardized tests than their peers. By ignoring this research, the English-only proponents imply that sound pedagogy does not matter.

I have been bilingual all of my speaking life. I know no other way. I do not know about English monolingualism, the speaking of *only* English. I do know, however, that speaking two languages has not lessened my patriotism to America or my allegiance to the flag. Nor has either language ever hindered my academic and life achievements, such as they are. Any failures in my life are generally attributable to other flaws in my whole character.

I am a speaker and listener of one of the first languages of this land—Cheyenne. I enjoy speaking this language with fellow Cheyenne speakers because embedded in this language are lessons that guide our daily lives and, thus, all that we are as human beings. We cannot leave behind the essence of our being. It cannot be legislated out of us, beaten out of us, nor snuffed to nothingness. The United States government and some schools have tried, but they have failed to suppress our language and destroy our culture.

For me, the Cheyenne language binds me to my reservation, my relatives, my culture, my fellow tribal members, and to life in general. This language forms an equally powerful bond between my wife and me, and she is non-Cheyenne and a monolingual

English speaker. She accepts the fact that my bilingualism is an essential part of who I am. Were it not for my bilingualism, I would not be the person she worships (I cannot resist a bit of humor).

Furthermore, Cheyenne is the language of our hallowed ancestors, our sacred rituals, our spiritualism, and our humor. It holds within it the respectful way I approach other people; the awed manner in which I say the place names of our sacred sites, like *Noavose* (our holy mountain near Sturgis, South Dakota); and the reverential way in which I talk to the creator. It contains the holy, serious, and humorous ways with which I interact with all people. Cheyenne is a language laden with laughter. My language gives me the psychological and emotional support to pursue my dreams. I do all this with my Cheyenne language.

Cheyenne and English Complementary

I am taking this opportunity to write about these multi-layered aspects of my language because I want children and non-speakers of the Cheyenne language to understand the metaphysical and metacognitive aspects of speaking another language. A bilingual person does not neatly dichotomize each language into separate compartments, nor are the languages automatically adversarial. The Cheyenne and English languages complement each other wonderfully. Speaking, reading, writing, and thinking in Cheyenne make me whole and enhance my life spiritually and intellectually. English enables me to make a living in the non-Cheyenne, English-speaking society and similarly enhances me spiritually and intellectually.

Both the Cheyenne and English languages have helped to form who I am, for good or bad. Both languages have helped me to achieve a modicum of success in the "White man's" world. Beyond the languages' utility, I take pleasure in reading, writing, and thinking in both languages.

I like reading and hearing the soaring words of Martin Luther King Jr., the solemn phraseology of the Lake Poets, the majesty and wit of Shakespeare, the whimsicality of Ogden Nash, and the inspiring obscurity of Dylan Thomas. I enjoy hearing the

Cheyenne lyrics and vocatives of our honor and flag songs. I like hearing the rhythmic, precise terminology of Cheyenne prayers. For me, both languages have equal weight and influence in all that I do.

I am writing about aspects of languages that transcend school curricula and patriotism. Apparently the promoters of English only do not fathom such a relationship with multiple languages.

Since one of our cultural values is to not draw attention to ourselves individually, I am writing with considerable discomfort in the first person singular, but I must because only I know my relationships to my two languages. However, I also know my thoughts and words convey the same sentiments, anger, and pain felt by thousands of other Native Americans.

But, as much as I hate to write this, I must acknowledge that the groups promoting English only also have the right to express themselves under the laws of this land. I would not seek to curtail that right. Voltaire said it best, and I paraphrase him here: I may not agree with what the promoters of English only advocate, but I will defend to the death their right to advocate it. I just wish the English-only group would understand our Declaration of Independence and Constitution and their guarantees. If they do not want to understand them the way we do, then they should at least acknowledge our basic human, psychological, emotional, and spiritual need to speak our non-English languages.

Hena'haanehe. That's all there is.

Richard Littlebear, EdD, has been president of Chief Dull Knife College on the Northern Cheyenne Indian Reservation in Montana since 1999.

"We Are Resilient, and We Are Succeeding"
A Statement before the Senate Committee on Indian Affairs

By Thomas Shortbull

Mr. Chairman and distinguished members of the committee, on behalf of my institution, Oglala Lakota College (OLC) in Kyle, South Dakota, and the 36 other tribal colleges and universities (TCUs) in the U.S. that compose the American Indian Higher Education Consortium (AIHEC), thank you for inviting me to testify at this hearing examining legislation to strengthen efforts to preserve and revitalize our Native languages.

My name is Thomas Shortbull. I am a member of the Oglala Lakota tribe, president of Oglala Lakota College, and a member of the board of directors of AIHEC. It is an honor to speak with the members of this committee about tribal colleges and the work we are doing to transform Indian Country. I am grateful to have this opportunity to recognize my good friend, Senator Tim Johnson with whom I served in the South Dakota State Senate in the mid-1980s, and to thank him for being a dedicated champion of the nation's tribal colleges and universities during his 28-year tenure in the United States Congress. I speak for all of the AIHEC member institutions in wishing him a retirement that is all he envisions and, indeed, deserves. He will be greatly missed.

Mr. Chairman, this afternoon I will speak about the tribal college movement and the legislation that is the subject of this hearing, including some recommendations that we are confident will advance our collective efforts to preserve and strengthen Native languages and culture. I ask that my statement, submitted on behalf of Oglala Lakota College and the American Indian Higher Education Consortium, be included in the hearing record.

Background of the Tribal College Movement

Mr. Chairman, you and the members of this committee have visited tribal colleges; you have walked on our campuses, met with

---

"'We Are Resilient, and We Are Succeeding': A Statement before the Senate Committee on Indian Affairs" was delivered June 18, 2014.

our leadership, and spent time with our students. All of this must have given you a fairly clear picture of the often tenuous financial situation facing many of our TCUs, when compared to state colleges and universities. Through visits to our campuses, you have gained an appreciation for the danger that inconsistent and inadequate funding presents to our efforts to attract and retain American Indian students and high quality faculty; to hire grant writers with the ability to compete against Research 1 institutions (as we are required to do); and to learn about and adopt the latest teaching, data collection, and management strategies required to maintain accreditation with regional accrediting bodies. These are issues we grapple with on a daily basis, even as we work to rebuild self-esteem and instill hope, a strong work ethic, and purposeful engagement within our students—many of whom have known little except lives of extreme poverty, unemployment, violence, abuse, and neglect.

We are doing all of this work and more in conditions that rival third world countries, amidst often dysfunctional governments and failing social systems, broken families, and oppression from both without and within. Yet, we are resilient, and we are succeeding. We are changing the lives and futures of students and their families for generations to come through a holistic and supportive educational environment that is culturally based and relevant to our students and their families. We are building stronger and more prosperous tribal nations through the restoration of our languages, community outreach programs and applied research on issues relevant to our land and our people, workforce training in fields critical to our reservation communities, and community-centered economic development and entrepreneurial programs. We are transforming our education systems—training early childhood educators, successfully managing once failing Head Start programs, rebuilding schoolhouses and children's lives, reforming K-12 science and math programs, providing summer and Saturday enrichment alternatives, preparing an American Indian K-12 teacher workforce, and transforming Native language instruction at all levels. We are growing a Native health care workforce, from behavioral health to emergency room nursing, to serve our people and provide care in our language and according to our customs.

We must be doing something right, because despite the lack of adequate funding and many other challenges we face, the tribal college movement has grown tremendously since Oglala Lakota College was established by my tribal leaders 43 years ago. To support our young and developing institutions, in 1973, Oglala Lakota College and the five other TCUs in existence at the time came together to establish AIHEC, enabling us to more effectively address the unmet higher education needs of American Indians and Indian Country.

Today, 37 tribal colleges operate more than 75 sites in 16 states. TCUs are located in the Plains, the Southwest, the Great Lakes, the Northwest, and even the North Slope of Alaska and have advanced American Indian higher education—and all Indian people—significantly since we first began in the late 1960s and early 1970s. Let me give you just one example: before Oglala Lakota College launched our nursing program, none of the nurses employed by the Indian Health Service to work on the Oglala reservation were American Indian. Today, more than 50% of the nurses on our reservation are American Indian and 85% of them are graduates of Oglala Lakota College.

Factors Contributing to Funding Challenges

Yet despite these advances, the lack of adequate funding that I mentioned earlier remains a serious obstacle to the sustainability, independence, and competitiveness of TCUs. A number of factors contribute to our ongoing funding challenges. While tribal colleges are public institutions, they are not state institutions, and consequently, we receive little or no state funding. In fact, very few states provide support for the non-Indian state residents attending TCUs, which account for about 20% of all tribal college students. However, if these same students attended a state institution, the state would be required to provide the institution with operational support for them. This is something we are trying to rectify through education and public policy change at the state and local level.

The tribal governments that have chartered tribal colleges are, for the most part, not among the handful of enormously wealthy gaming tribes located near major urban areas that one reads about in the mass media. Rather, they are some of the poorest governments in the nation. In fact, seven of the 10 poorest counties in America are home to a tribal college.

Finally, the federal government, despite its trust responsibility, binding treaty obligations, and the exchange of more than one billion acres of land, has never fully funded our primary institutional operations source, the Tribally Controlled Colleges and Universities Assistance Act (TCU Act), and overall funds TCUs at levels far below that of other institutions of higher education. Today, the TCU Act is appropriated at about $5,850 per full-time Indian student, which after more than 30 years is still only about 73% of the level authorized by Congress to operate these tribal institutions. Faced with ever rising costs of day-to-day operations, to continue to thrive and expand as community-based institutions, TCUs must stabilize, sustain, and increase our basic operational funding. While our per student funding is higher than it has been at times in the past, it is still considerably lower than the operating support received by other public four-year institutions, which is the direction that many TCUs are evolving. In fact, 13 TCUs currently offer several bachelor's degrees each, and five, including Oglala Lakota College, offer master's degrees.

Tribal Colleges are first and foremost academic institutions, but because of the number of challenges facing Indian Country—high unemployment, poorly developed economies, poor health status, and lack of stable community infrastructures—tribal colleges are called upon to do much more than provide higher education services. Tribal colleges often run entrepreneurial and business development centers; many TCUs are the primary GED and adult basic education provider on their reservations; and most if not all TCUs offer a variety of educational and training programs for tribal employees, BIA and IHS staff, K-12 schools, tribal courts and justice system staff, and many others in a manner to suit their work schedules. TCUs run daycare centers, elementary immersion schools, Head Start programs, health nutrition education programs, community gardens, and often the only community library and tribal museum or archives. Mr. Chairman, tribal colleges are by any definition engaged institutions, intricately woven into the fabric of our respective communities.

Reauthorizing the Native American Programs Act of 1974 to Ensure the Survival and Vitality of Native American Languages

We strongly support this reauthorization, and we urge the Committee to work toward its enactment this year. Tribal colleges are actively and aggressively working to preserve and sustain our tribal language and culture. All TCUs offer Native language courses. In some cases, the tribal language would have been completely lost if not for the local tribal college. Turtle Mountain Community College in Belcourt, North Dakota, was established primarily for this purpose, and over the years its success in writing and revitalizing the Turtle Mountain Chippewa language has been truly remarkable. Aaniiih Nakoda College in Montana runs a K-6 language immersion school, right on campus. At the White Clay Immersion School, children learn the White Clay language and culture in addition to subjects they would routinely study at any other school. Oglala Lakota College does the same, operating the successful Lakota Language Immersion School for kindergarten through 5th grade, next door to our main campus. Other TCUs are teaching and providing care in our Native language to our youngest children, as a regular part of the college's daycare program for infants and toddlers.

Additionally, many TCUs offer unique associate and bachelor degree programs that include Native language instruction, as well as in-service teacher training in language and culture. At the TCUs, teacher education programs follow cultural protocols and stress the use of Native language in everyday instruction.

Some committee members might wonder why tribal colleges, as academic institutions of higher education, would be focusing on language revitalization, running Head Start and daycare programs, and establishing our own elementary immersion schools. Why? Because we are holistic institutions. TCUs focus on the whole student—mind, body, spirit, family, and community. We know that just as we are succeeding in higher education, we can put our minds together and implement strategies of success for our babies and children. Where others might fail, we have the commitment and the stability to succeed.

Several years ago, we began to notice a troubling trend at Oglala Lakota College: every year, fewer and fewer of our entering students were fluent in or could even speak our Lakota language. The vast majority of these students had attended schools in the local area, some of them taking Lakota language courses for 8, 10, or even 12 years. Yet, their mastery of the Lakota language was missing. They could recite a few words [like] *ina-ahte* (mother-father), some simple phrases, sing a few Lakota songs, and count *wáŋči-wikčémna* (1-10). The sad fact is that on my reservation, language instruction in the K-12 schools has not produced any language speakers over the last 40 years. Even more troubling, we conducted our own survey within our local communities and learned that while 70-80% of our elders could speak Lakota, only about 5% of our tribe's 4 to 6-year-olds could speak the language.

We at Oglala Lakota College knew that if our people had any hope for reversing this trend, it was up to our college. The responsibility and, what's more, the will to act was ours. It was time for OLC to open our own elementary school.

Oglala Lakota College applied for and received the first of two three-year grants from the Department of Health and Human Services' Administration on Native Americans. Because of the depth and complexity of the language issues facing our people, we spent most of the first three years of our project researching different methods for achieving greater Lakota language proficiency. We opened our Lakota school teaching about one-half of the curricula in Lakota and the other half in English. However, after studying other elementary education programs, including highly successful Maori and Native Hawaiian programs, as well as monitoring the progress of our own students, we realized that to maximize our effectiveness and make systemic change, an immersion program is the solution. Last fall, in the second year of grant two, our Lakota Immersion School provided Lakota language immersion instruction to our K-5 students.

Based on our experience at Oglala Lakota College, we have two recommendations for this committee: (1) to achieve significant results that will truly impact the future of our people, the Department of Health and Human Services Administration for Native Americans (DHHS-ANA) language grant program should be modified. Rather than awarding grants for a period of three years, grants should be awarded for a period of 10 years. Alternatively, DHHS-ANA could adopt the model used with success by the National Science Foundation. NSF currently makes awards under its tribal college and university program for a period of five years, with the option to award an additional five-year grant upon demonstration of adequate progress. NSF has determined that to address systemic challenges, sustainable funding for at least 10 years is needed. (2) Because of the extensive work that Oglala Lakota College and the other TCUs are already doing to determine the most effective strategies for teaching our children and preserving our endangered languages, and more important, to expand this urgent work, a TCU research grant program should be included in the Native Language Immersion Student Achievement Act. Such a program would enable TCUs to continue to work to identify the best language pedagogy to achieve systemic change and ensure the survival and revival of our Native languages.

Indeed, Mr. Chairman, we believe that you understand the critical need for this type of program because in both the 110th and 111th Congresses you included such a provision in legislation you sponsored known as "The Path." This legislation was developed to support the work of TCUs in Native language research and practice; health professions workforce development; and Native health and wellness research and programs. We strongly urge you to include the Native language provisions of The Path. It is vital that TCUs be included in this legislation, which currently excludes us.

Mr. Chairman and Senator Johnson, thank you for this opportunity to share our story, successes, and concerns with you today. We look forward to enactment of legislation to advance the preservation and revitalization of our Native languages and to a day when all Americans—including the first Americans—seeking to further their education and career goals have full and fair chance at success.

Thomas Shortbull is president of Oglala Lakota College.

"To Revitalize Our Languages, We Must Work at All Levels"
A Statement before the U.S. Senate Committee on Indian Affairs

By Clarena M. Brockie

Mr. Chairman and distinguished members of the committee, my name is Clarena M. Brockie, and I am Aaniiih (Gros Ventre) from Montana. Both of my parents are enrolled Gros Ventre. I am proud to represent Montana's 32nd district, which includes the Fort Belknap and Rocky Boy Indian Reservations, in our state's House of Representatives. I am also the Dean of Students of Aaniiih Nakoda College (ANC) in Harlem, Montana. Aaniiih Nakoda College was chartered by the Fort Belknap Indian Community Council in 1984. We are a small school with a big mission, serving approximately 225 students per semester—most of whom are members of one of the two tribes on our reservation.

Thank for inviting me to testify at this hearing examining legislation to strengthen efforts to preserve and revitalize our Native languages. It is an honor to be given an opportunity to speak on behalf of the many people who cannot stand here today, but I know they are with me in spirit. Aaniiih Nakoda College, along with the nation's other 36 tribal colleges and universities (TCUs), which collectively are the American Indian Higher Education Consortium (AIHEC), support S. 1948 and S. 2299, both of which would help us as we work to ensure the survival and continuing vitality of Native American languages.

Current Status of Native Languages

The Committee knows the dire situation we face as Indian people in terms of the loss of our languages, homelands, and identity, so I will not recite all of the statistics. I will just mention that when Christopher Columbus and other Europeans first came to Indian

---

"'To Revitalize Our Languages, We Must Work at All Levels': A Statement before the U.S. Senate Committee on Indian Affairs" was delivered on June 18, 2014.

Country, more than 300 different languages were spoken here. Today, well less than half remain. Most of these are spoken only by a handful of elders and are in serious danger of disappearing. In fact, all but 15 or 20 of our Native languages are spoken only by adults who are not teaching their younger generations the language. This tragic outcome is a direct result of prior U.S. government policies, including assimilation which sent many Indian children to government-run boarding schools where they were prohibited from, and often fiercely punished for, speaking their own languages—their last tie to their homelands and their very identity.

This terrible legacy is made even worse when you consider that once a language becomes extinct it takes with it much of the history, philosophy, ceremonies, culture, and environmental and scientific knowledge of the people who spoke it. It is difficult to imagine the degree to which such a loss will impact our Indian children and young people who are already suffering from generational poverty and oppression, violence, abuse and neglect, lack of self-esteem, and, most tragic, lack of hope.

Fortunately, over the past few decades, greater attention has been focused on the need to preserve our Native culture and language, and a few modest pieces of legislation have been enacted at the federal level, including the Native American Languages Act of 1990 and the inadequately funded Esther Martinez Native American Languages Preservation Act of 2006.

The Survival of Native Languages

My graduate school thesis focused on the oral history of the Gros Ventre, and in the process of conducting research, I learned how meticulously and systematically our own Gros Ventre language had been removed from our homes and schools. We were even prohibited from conducting our ceremonies. The Aaniiih nin (White Clay People) became one of the many tribes that was in danger of joining the group of "vanishing Indians." In the early 1600s, there were more than 15,000 Aaniiih nin, but by 1903, there were less than 300.

In 1997, the Aaniiih language, which is one of two Native languages spoken on the Fort Belknap reservation, was in the last stages of survival. Only 25 speakers existed, and no children—kindergarten through 12th grade—spoke the language. But despite the grim predictions and statistics, the Aaniiih nin have survived. Today, our language is beginning to thrive with more young language speakers, thanks to an important project at Aaniiih Nakoda College.

In the late 1990s, I was employed by Aaniiih Nakoda College (then called Fort Belknap College) as the development officer, and we decided it was time to write a planning grant proposal for a project to try to revive our language. At ANC, students are required to take language and tribal history classes for one or both tribes. In addition, Aaniiih and Nakoda language and culture classes are taught in the local public high schools and evening classes are held for community members who want to learn the Aaniiih and Nakoda languages. A speaker-learner project was also pursued. However, none of these efforts achieved the level of fluency we needed to ensure the continued vitality of our language into the future. It seemed that to be truly successful, the Native language needed to be spoken consistently in the home and at school. Without some kind of consistent reinforcement, many students retain only a portion of the words taught. I wrote the grant proposal, entitled "Speaking White Clay," with all of this in mind, and we prepared it with input and support from the Gros Ventre cultural committee and Native language speakers.

Fortunately for us, the funder stressed the need to focus on our youth and asked in the review process, "What are you doing for the youth?" The goal of our grant was to ensure the survival and continuing vitality of our language and culture. With a funded plan, Aaniiih Nakoda College President Dr. Carole Falcon Chandler, along with staff and faculty, set out to fulfill the dream of our elders to protect our language.

After researching the issue, we determined that our best hope for success was in the establishment of a full day immersion program. In 2003, Dr. Janine Pease, who conducted an extensive study of Native American language immersion initiatives entitled,

"Native American Language Immersion: Innovative Native Education for Children and Families,"[1] wrote, "Most intriguing about the Native and Indigenous language immersion models is the clear and positive connection between Native and Indigenous language and culture with educational achievement. . . For indigenous people, Native American language immersion activities hold great promise in the development of children, youth, family, and community."

Establishment of the White Clay Immersion School

In 2003, the White Clay Immersion School was established under the Aaniiih Nakoda College.[2] The goals of the school are to: (1) promote the survival and vitality of the White Clay language; (2) provide culturally based educational opportunities that build cognitive skills and foster academic success; (3) instill self-esteem and positive cultural identify; and (4) prepare students to become productive members of society.

Unfortunately, since we wrote our proposal in 1997, we have lost our oldest Native speakers. Today, no fluent elder Aaniiih speaker lives on the Fort Belknap reservation. There are a few younger people who have learned the language and speak it well. However, today the largest generation of Aaniiih speakers comprises the students of Aaniiih Nakoda College's White Clay Immersion School (WCIS). Since WCIS began, child Native speakers have grown from none to 30. Students at WCIS attend a full day of classes in an immersion setting. Teaching and learning focus on the White Clay language and rely heavily on Native knowledge and Native ways of knowing and being. Non-Native ways of learning are incorporated to offer students the best of both worlds and to help them become positive and successful members

---

[1] See Pease, "Native American Language Immersion Innovative Native Education for Children and Families," pp. 153-215.

[2] For an in-depth look at WCIS, see Umbhau, "Firing Up White Clay: Immersion School Students Encouraged to Return, Give Back," 127-130; and Paskus, "More than Words, A Way of Life: Language Restoration Program Reach Beyond Tribal Colleges and Universities," pp. 38-46.

of the larger community. WCIS's curriculum emphasizes the interconnections between physical, mental, and spiritual well-being through cross-disciplinary integration, intergenerational learning, and field-based learning experiences. Students participate in community projects, public events, and international exchanges.

The White Clay Immersion School is the first, and now one of two, full-day Native language immersion schools operating within a tribal college. Oglala Lakota College in Kyle, South Dakota, operates the other immersion school through grade 5. WCIS now includes both elementary and middle school. The school is housed in the beautiful Aaniiih Nakoda Cultural Building. This unique and innovative partnership in educational self-determination serves as a transformative model for other American Indian communities across the United States that are facing the impending loss of their own Native language.

Administrative Leadership and Quality of WCIS Staff

The White Clay Immersion School operates within Aaniiih Nakoda College's central administration under the direction of the college president. Dr. Lynette Chandler serves as the director of White Clay Immersion School since its inception in 2002. She has extensive knowledge of and training in immersion teaching practices and has worked with Indigenous language experts from Montana, Wyoming, Hawaii, Peru, Guatemala, Australia, and New Zealand. Dr. Chandler earned her BS (English) and MA (Native American Studies) at Montana State University, and her EdD (Educational Leadership) at the University of Montana. Her accolades include being named "Montana Indian Educator" in 2012 and awarded the Andrew W. Mellon Foundation Career Enhancement Fellowship from the American Indian College Fund. In 2008, the White Clay Immersion School received the commissioner's Outstanding Project Award from the Administration for Native Americans.

Two of the classroom instructors have graduated from the Office of Indian Education Teacher Training Program. Both of the

Aaniiih language teachers have their doctorate degrees and are fluent in Aaniiih.

Success and Academic Achievement for WCIS Students

Graduates from the White Clay Immersion School have transitioned to public schools and are recognized by these schools as leaders in student government, academics, and sports. For example, students graduating from WCIS in 2013 are now sophomores at a local off-reservation public school. Last year, two students from the White Clay Immersion School received the science award, math award, English award, literature award, and art award for their grade at their new, off-reservation high school. They also excelled in athletics, receiving the varsity basketball awards and were on the honor roll throughout the school year.

Of those from WCIS's original 2011 graduating class who have gone on to local public schools, three of the four students have been inducted into the National Honor Society. All four are on the honor roll; they excel in sports and are involved in community activities; they work after school and will be employed this summer. All of these students will be seniors in fall 2014.

For the last three years, these students have been at the forefront of leadership within their school. They are on the student council; participate in Jobs for Montana Graduates, Indian Club, yearbook, volunteer programs, and lead the class awards at the end of school year. Two of three students who have graduated from WCIS in 2012 have been inducted into the National Honor Society and all are on the honor roll. They have received numerous awards in high school and are working summer jobs currently for the City of Harlem. These students excel in their specific clubs; are managers on sports teams; and excel in track, basketball, and volleyball. They volunteer in the community or school on a regular basis.

Financial Security for WCIS

Financial support for the White Clay Immersion School has been sporadic. The bulk of funding has come from private foundations and local support. In addition, we have received funding from the U.S. Department of Health and Human Services' (DHHS) Administration of Native American (ANA) program. However, this is a competitive program and in some years, WCIS has not been funded.

WCIS does not receive funding from the state or any federal formula funding. Instead, the staff hosts fundraisers to support school trips, lunches, supplies and other school activities. Although it is a struggle at times, Aaniiih Nakoda College remains committed to our goal for the survival of our Aaniiih language, and we remain committed to all current and future students of the White Clay Immersion School who hold the future of our people in their hands and hearts. Grounded in their culture and confident in their language, we know that through them our people and our language will thrive for many generations to come.

Other Successful Native Language Models: TCUs Lead the Way

Despite the documented need and proven value, funding for language immersion and revitalization programs has been particularly problematic for American Indian people, particularly because funding sources are categorical: [they] have specific departmental priorities, extreme dollar limitations, and are short-term. A study conducted by Dr. Janine Pease, and discussed above, reports on 50 language immersion projects in Indian Country and documents the serious challenges language programs have in acquiring sustained support. American Indian language revitalization programs are a difficult fit for programs most often designed for other language groups, Hispanic-serving schools, colleges, and communities. Language programs, [which rely on] several federal agencies, have a severe limitation in funding, making competition stiff and discouraging applications altogether. Grant terms of three to five years limit the language programs sustainability, thereby limiting language learning as well. Granting agencies have little or no support for planning or start-up costs.

Despite these difficulties, some excellent programs are in place at tribal colleges, which can serve as models for others.

- Little Big Horn College and Fort Peck Community College in Montana have developed a tribal languages acquisition program using the Plains Indian Sign Language as the means for learning and using 400 terms and phrases in the Crow, Nakona (Assiniboine), and Dakota languages. This initiative has classroom strategies, a DVD for viewing at home on the TV, and a CD for listening in the car or on mobile listening devices.

- The Piegan Institute of Browning, Montana, developed three K-8 language immersion schools: Cuts Wood, Moccasin Flat, and Lost Child. The schools instruct all subjects in the Blackfeet language. Founder Darrell Kipp says, "The school's graduates are the first young fluent speakers of the Blackfeet language in a generation…the school is not only resuscitating the language, but also help to preserve Blackfeet culture."

- At Turtle Mountain Community College in Belcourt, North Dakota, a key institutional goal is for all college employees to engage in 100 hours of language instruction, with 20% of staff reaching fluency.

- Aaniiih Nakoda College and six other TCUs in Montana have collaborated in the Learning Lodge Institute to develop best practices in language teaching and to create a certification process to enable language instructors to teach in public school classrooms.

- Oglala Lakota College, in Kyle, South Dakota, has also established a successful K-5 Lakota language immersion school, while also working to expand the number and effectiveness of language instructors through interdepartmental collaboration [between] Lakota Studies and teacher training programs.

As these examples demonstrate, preserving, revitalizing, and teaching Native languages are fundamental priorities of the nation's tribal colleges. In fact, many were established specifically to protect and preserve a tribe's language. Over the years, the TCUs have broadened their programming beyond college-aged students to impact younger children.

Closing Recommendations

Mr. Chairman, I join President Shortbull and all of the tribal colleges in making these recommendations: (1) Include Senator Tester's TCU language research provisions. The Committee should include the important tribal college Native language research and education programs, which he included in legislation he introduced in the 110 and 111th Congresses as part of The Path legislation, as an amendment to S. 1948. To revitalize our languages, we must work at all levels, pre-K to college, and we must continue to expand critically needed Native language research. More support is needed for Native language immersion programs, classes, community-based programs, and enrichment activities. However, equally important is the need to invest wisely in research and pedagogy and [study] how Native language use improves the academic achievement of Native American students. Tribal colleges simply cannot continue to be asked to do more with less. (2) Increase ANA language grant periods. To achieve significant results that will truly impact the future of our people, the DHHS-ANA language grant program should be modified. Rather than awarding grants for a period of three years, grants should be awarded for a period of 10 years. Alternatively, DHHS-ANA could adopt the model used with success by the National

Science Foundation. NSF currently makes awards under its tribal college and university program for a period of five years, with the option to award an additional five-year grant upon a demonstration of adequate progress. NSF has determined that to address systemic challenges, sustainable funding for at least 10 years is needed.

In closing, I will simply echo words of frustration, which I heard from many members of the committee during your hearing last week on American Indian higher education. It is so incredibly frustrating to know that the need is so very great and the models of success exist; to know that tribal colleges—more so than any other entities—are working every day to transform Indian Country, achieving success but being rewarded only with flat-line or decreased funding; to be asked by our people, the administration, and Congress to do more and more with less and less. We are accountable institutions. We need the administration to be accountable as well.

Mr. Chairman, our struggles will continue. We need your help and that of the administration—not just to acknowledge the existence of treaties and the federal trust responsibility, but to take concrete action—starting right now—to advance the proven successes of the tribal colleges and increase our capacity to do even more for the betterment of Indian Country. Thank you.

Clarena M. Brockie is the dean of students at Aaniiih Nakoda College and served as a member of the Montana House of Representatives.

Native Languages Preserve Our Way of Thinking and Knowing

By Richard B. Williams

Recently, I had an exceptional opportunity to facilitate a convening of several "Native language doyens." A Native language doyen is a leading figure who works tirelessly in language programs and activities in our Native communities. It was very stirring to see the spiritual essence that comes from our cultural language guardians who are reintroducing and saving our precious languages. The doyens—through their diligent hard work—are producing fluent Native speakers throughout Indian Country.

During my lifetime, I've heard elders and medicine people eloquently and profoundly say that our languages are sacred. I never really understood what that meant until I had the opportunity to spend time thoroughly immersed in the Lakota language. The experience left me in awe of what it meant to learn a language. My first experience of understanding that the language was sacred came when, in a dream, I was speaking Lakota. The second experience was when I was cognitively processing the world around me in Lakota, not English. I remember looking at this *sunka* and I realized that in my mind I used that term instead of dog. After that profound experience I would naturally and without dual cognitive processing see objects in Lakota and not in English.

The mysterious part of understanding that a language is sacred had nothing to do with the way we were learning the language. We weren't meditating nor were we praying constantly. We weren't asking the Creator to help us learn the language. We were just simply immersed and totally focused on learning and experiencing the language. There was never really an "ah-ha" moment where I felt that somehow the experience was sacred. It was an inner sense of knowing our people and the speaking of the language allowed our people to live in harmony and in a sacred

"Native Languages Preserve Our Way of Thinking and Knowing" appeared in *First Nations News*, January 18, 2018.

way. The profound nature of the experience has changed me and heightened my path to learning more of the language and, even more importantly, to understand the inviolability of visions and dreams. The unconscious act of dreaming in Lakota was a significant spiritual experience. One of the sacred ceremonies of the Lakota is the *hanblecha*, or vision quest, and dreams have always been a very important connection to the spirit world and Creator. There is no English word to express this feeling. In Lakota we understand it as *Wakan*—a great mystery.

The opportunity to spend time with the language doyens was inspirational. Their knowledge of the language and its acquisition was complex, and each person had different ways to accomplish the goal of creating fluency among their people, especially in the children. The lifetime commitment made by each of the participants is notable. We had participants who were relatively young, as well as seasoned language veterans. An important message from each participant was that Native language acquisition and Western methodological educational practices are not symbiotic. Contemporary education practices that exist in schools today do not work well, and there is a wealth of American Indian experts and current teachers who are very critical of the Western methodology and pedagogy. The message was clear: do not malign language immersion by force fitting it into existing education practices.

Language acquisition is important because in practice it has been demonstrated in studies and in practitioners' testimony that it improves and enhances a child's confidence and self-image. It is well documented that increasing a child's self-worth is one of the most important aspects to their future success. The research also indicates that when the educational experience is culturally and language-based, it produces a greater sense of wellbeing in a child. This knowledge is so compelling that it should behoove and compel all educational practitioners to alter their work to include language and cultural activities in their daily practices. The caution here is the reminder that the contemporary education system is failing our students, and we will only be successful if we make a complete change to the existing archaic way our children are being taught.

The second compelling reason for language in our schools has to do with enhanced cognitive development. Second-language speakers become better students because they are learning to process information in different parts of their brains. The cognition of language acquisition enhances critical thinking and improved learning intelligence. Recently it has been reported that it is good for the old folks. Learning a second language as an adult can help one avoid cognitive decline, and it is reported that bilinguals come down with dementia and Alzheimer's more than four years later than monolinguals. Although I regretfully inform you that age limits the ability to learn the language even if you were a child who spoke the language fluently.

Other advantages inherent in speaking a Native language is that it introduces new words, concepts, metaphors and timeframes. People who speak multiple languages tend to score higher on standardized tests in subjects such as math, reading, and vocabulary.

We are living in a world that is foreign to us and would not be recognized by our ancestors. As we continue to adjust to the challenges of this changing world, it is comforting to know that to hold on to our languages means that we will continue to preserve our way of thinking and knowing. It is that sacred language and our good ways that will help us secure a place in this world, forever!

Richard B. Williams is Oglala Lakota and the former CEO and president of the American Indian College Fund.

PROFILES

The growth of tribal colleges and universities over the past 50 years has facilitated the expansion of Indigenous language courses and programs. While informed by curricular trends elsewhere, individual TCUs have harnessed available resources to develop their own unique programming to best serve their respective student populations. The result has been myriad programs, tailored teaching strategies, and trailblazing projects.

As part of its editorial mission, *Tribal College Journal* has served as a platform for the tribal colleges to share their stories and to exchange information on language revitalization strategies, both generally and specifically. In the spring of 2000, TCJ's editor, Marjane Ambler, pulled together the journal's first issue devoted completely to Native language. Most of the articles were profiles of various programs at different TCUs. "Rekindling the Anishnabe Language Fires at Bay Mills" focused on that tribal college's Nishnaabemowin Language Instructors' Institute which offered intensive six-week summer sessions to prepare language instructors. Similarly, "Using Blackfoot Language to Rediscover Who We Are," authored by Duane Mistaken Chief Sr., shared the philosophy and strategy behind Red Crow Community College's Niitsi-tapi Teacher Education Project. And "Little Priest Immerses Students in Language," offered a concise overview of that TCU's three-week summer workshop.

Founding TCJ editor, Paul Boyer, wrote the issue's centerpiece feature: "Learning Lodge Institute: Montana Colleges Empower Cultures to Save Languages," which illuminated how one collaborative project brought together all seven of Montana's TCUs despite the state's great linguistic diversity. Each college developed its own individual courses and curriculum, but they came together periodically to share their stories and to offer mutual support.

The Learning Lodge Institute was just one of many unique language revitalization programs developed by educators at TCUs in the early 2000s. In the article, "Giving Voice to Crow Country: The Crow Place Name Project," elders and faculty at Little Big Horn College created a mapping project that documented traditional Crow names for places and other geographical landmarks. Truly underscoring the inextricable connection between culture and language, the project also recorded the Crow stories and history behind the names, all the while utilizing geographic information systems (GIS) to precisely locate each landmark. Readers can discover further efforts to reclaim Crow in the article, "Teasing Aside: Little Big Horn College Maintains Crow Language, Culture."

In part, the Crow Place Name Project was made possible due to the relative vitality of the Crow language. Other Indigenous languages in the northern Plains and Rocky Mountains, however, have been facing near-collapse. Aaniiih was one such language, leading Aaniiih Nakoda College (ANC) to lead revitalization efforts with its Speaking White Clay Project. In 2004, Ron Selden chronicled the project in his article, "Back from the Brink: Innovative Language Program Involves Three Generations." Due to the tireless work of the late Lynette Chandler and her husband Sean, ANC's project eventually metamorphosed into the White Clay Immersion School, which continues to immerse children in the Aaniiih language. The article, "Firing Up White Clay: Immersion School Students Encouraged to Return, Give Back," traces that metamorphosis.

Readers can also follow the evolution of language revitalization at Bay Mills Community College in the article, "Language of the People Forever: Bay Mills Spins Thread Tying Ojibwa Communities Together," which serves as a sequel of sorts to "Rekindling the Anishnabe Language Fires at Bay Mills." BMCC's "Nishnaabemwin Pane Immersion School evolved out of the college's instructor's institute. Author Brenda Austin discusses the program and illuminates the tremendous amount of work and effort that goes into language revitalization, both for learners and teachers.

In 2013, 13 years after its inaugural issue on Native language, TCJ published a second issue devoted to revitalization efforts at

TCUs. Laura Paskus' "More than Words, a Way of Life," (found in the Overviews section of this book) headlined a handful of articles on the topic. Persia Erdrich's "Ojibwemotaadidaa: Preparing a New Generation of Fluent Speakers," gave a firsthand account of Fond du Lac Tribal and Community College's summer immersion program, while Mary Weasel Fat's "Louis Soop and Language Restoration at Red Crow Community College" focused on how that tribal college makes use of elders and traditional knowledge. Two other pieces, "Iḷisaġvik College Offers Language Nest Program" and "Blackfeet Community College Develops Language App" give concise overviews of efforts at those TCUs.

As evidenced by Blackfeet Community College's strides and the development of other Native language apps and computer programs, technology can play a powerful role in language revitalization and preservation. Jurgita Antoine, who has taught at both Sinte Gleska University and Sisseton Wahpeton College, discusses a digitization project that seeks to preserve the Lakota language for posterity in her article, "Lakota Documentaries: Working with Cultural Heritage at a Tribal University." Published in *Anthropology News*, this article from 2014 traces how the late Sinte Gleska University professor Don Moccasin teamed up with some tech savvy staffers at SGU to record and digitize elders speaking in their Indigenous language. The university has used the recordings for instruction and has turned the transcripts into Lakota language texts. It's an empowering process, Antoine states, "The elders became more comfortable with technology and Lakota orthography, while the younger participants were learning Lakota language and culture."

In comparison to many Native languages, Lakota is relatively robust, a point made by Arman Murphy, who served as an intern at the Lakota Language Consortium. For over a decade the consortium has hosted the Lakota Summer Institute at Oglala Lakota College and Sitting Bull College. In this final program profile, Christopher Vondracek, a writer for the *Rapid City Journal*, offers an overview of the institute and the inroads it has made.

Learning Lodge Institute
Montana Colleges Empower Cultures to Save Languages

By Paul Boyer

In the kitchen of a reservation home an elderly woman is preparing dinner. By her side, a young child—her grandson—watches and helps. The grandmother asks for ingredients: flour, water, maybe some salt or sugar. The boy gathers each and returns. The grandmother thanks him, and the boy smiles in reply.

It is a quiet and perhaps common scene, but for many Native American educators, one important question remains unanswered: what language are the two speaking? Are they conversing in English? Or are they speaking the traditional language of their own tribe? The answer does not simply complete this imagined family picture but says something important about the strength of language in a tribal community. Ultimately, it may say something important about the ability of that tribe to sustain itself as a distinct people.

Crow. Blackfeet. Kootenai. Assiniboine. Salish. Cree. Gros Ventre. Northern Cheyenne. These are names of tribal groups residing in what is now the state of Montana. They are, in every case, also distinct languages or dialects. On each of the state's seven reservations, language and culture are inseparably bound together and, according to Montana tribal college educators, one cannot survive without the other.

But more than 150 years of sustained contact with non-Indian culture has taken its toll on these and other languages. The enforcement of English in boarding schools in the 19th and early 20th centuries helped speed the process of erosion, leaving many children unable to speak ancient languages with fluency and ashamed of parents who did. More recently, increased contact with non-Indians and American popular culture through radio, television, and now the internet, causes further marginalization of

"Learning Lodge Institute: Montana Colleges Empower Cultures to Save Languages" appeared in *Tribal College: Journal of American Indian Higher Education, 11*(3), in spring 2000.

tribal languages, even on reservations where the language is relatively strong.

In response, educators and community activists across the state are making what is the first coordinated effort to rebuild language fluency within their reservations. The Learning Lodge Institute, as the project is called, is a collaboration of all seven Montana tribal colleges. Each institution develops and directs projects that best serve the needs of their own reservation community. But they also gather periodically to share what they have learned, support each other's efforts, and get inspiration from Indigenous peoples as far away as Hawaii and New Zealand.

The Learning Lodge Institute is partially funded by the W.K. Kellogg Foundation, as part of a major, multi-year initiative to support Native American higher education, and tribal colleges in particular. Little Big Horn College on the Crow reservation is the lead institution, distributing $850,000 over a four-year period.

The goal is to "use education for the teaching of language and culture," said project director Lanny Real Bird. This dual mission is key: more than language courses, the Learning Lodge Institute promotes projects that also strengthen knowledge of traditional culture. Individual projects include the certification of language teachers, documentation of medical and ceremonial plants, development of language handbooks, sponsorship of culturally based immersion programs, and creation of partnerships with Head Start classrooms and public schools.

All this helps tribal communities reach a larger goal, said Real Bird. It is part of each college's mission to "empower the cultures so they can empower themselves," he said. This means directing "their own education, their own health, their own government. To utilize their own resources." Language instruction is therefore not an exercise in sentimentality but part of a strategy for self-determination.

Documenting the Loss of Language

It is obvious to even a casual visitor that tribal language is no longer the *lingua franca* within many of Montana's reservation communities. In the streets, stores, government offices, and schools, English usually dominates. But it is difficult to document language loss with precision. Many tribal members have some knowledge of the language. But comprehension may be restricted to a few words or remembered phrases.

"A lot of people say they understand the language," said Richard Littlebear, president of Dull Knife Memorial College[1] on the Northern Cheyenne Reservation. "Actually, I don't think they do because when the gestures and body language are taken away, many can't really comprehend the language without these hints."

Language survival requires a strong cadre of fluent speakers, people who use the language with confidence. But fluency is increasingly rare. Tribal educators are often hesitant to estimate exact numbers, but on many reservations educated guesses range from the single digits to low hundreds.

On the Blackfeet reservation in northwest Montana, for example, Marvin Weatherwax estimates that about 350 people understand the language, but "very few, if any" are truly fluent. On the Fort Belknap Reservation, meanwhile, 16 fluent Assiniboine speakers were located in 1994. Fourteen Gros Ventre speakers were identified on that reservation in 1996.

On other reservations, fluency is more common. On the Crow reservation, the Crow language is still heard in public spaces—including Little Big Horn College. But here, too, its status is threatened. A decade ago, I was told that over 80% of Crows could speak their language. But in a recent interview, Learning Lodge Institute director Lanny Real Bird doubted that this figure was still accurate and referred to the "handful" of fluent speakers remaining.

On all reservations, the concern is not simply about the limited numbers of speakers. More worrisome is the advanced age of the speakers. I was repeatedly told that the language is dying with the elders. On the Fort Peck reservation, the Dakota and Nakota languages were declared linguistically "obsolete" in 1997 because

---

[1] Dull Knife Memorial College changed its name to Chief Dull Knife College in 2001.

no fluent speaker younger than 37 could be found. On the Blackfeet reservation, 505 fluent speakers were identified in 1994. In that same year, however, 102 of those speakers died.

This loss of elders prompts a sense of urgency and helps explain development of the Language Lodge Institute. Tribal educators say that language survival cannot be put off—it must happen now while there are still elders willing to teach the language or support the world of classroom teacher and college faculty.

Building Support for Tribal Languages

Richard Littlebear gave the image of the grandmother and grandson talking together in the home as we sat in his paneled office at Dull Knife Memorial College. With a mischievous smile, he had just offered a long, lyrical Cheyenne word of his own creation for "computer." His point was that the Cheyenne language is still relevant. The real threat, he said, is that too few tribal members appreciate how endangered it is or have faith that it can be revived.

The elder and child symbolize the fragility of language and how its future may, in a very real way, be determined by the interaction between the two. If the grandmother speaks her language, and the child listens and responds, there is hope. But what happens when the grandmother uses English with the boy or, more poignant still, quickly reverts to English when he doesn't understand her words?

Littlebear said elders don't always know how much is at stake or feel they have a role to play. Meanwhile, the young may feel that they cannot learn the language. "A lot think that teaching the language is not possible," he said.

There is also a persistent belief that past failures to restore language guarantee future failure. "That is the difficulty," asserted Lanny Real Bird, who recently completed a doctoral degree from Montana State University. Scattered across his desk are copies of language videos, cassette tapes, and textbooks developed by tribes across the state, suggesting that a strong and sustained language movement exists. But too many tribal members are conditioned to believe that language training is another temporary, fly-by-night project.

"We have an attitude in the community: 'Is this another program that will be here today and gone tomorrow?'"

Multiple Approaches

Tribal college leaders say the answer is "no." Many tribal colleges already have language instruction programs in place. The purpose of the Learning Lodge is to support these existing programs, make them stronger and, especially, better connected to the culture and community. By building on what already exists, time and money are used most efficiently, and programs have a better chance of living on when the initiative ends.

The results of this unique approach can be seen on the Flathead reservation. Here, Salish Kootenai College has a long-standing language program that teaches both Salish and Kootenai. Yet results were disappointing, said Vernon Finley, coordinator of the Learning Lodge Institute on campus. "Not one fluent speaker has been produced by any program here," he asserted. "It's not a lack of desire," he added, "but a lack of an appropriate curriculum."

Introductory courses are not enough, said Finley. Students must be able to both study and live the language. They need more than vocabulary lists. Exposure to fluent speakers who can also make connections to the tribe's culture is essential. For this reason, Finley argues that elders must play a central role in any language program. At this college, the Learning Lodge Institute allowed the college to hire elders to help develop language curriculum materials.

A Culture Leadership Program is also giving a select group of students a more intensive, culturally based approach to language instruction. In this innovative program, a small group of tribal members spend a year working with Salish elder Johnny Arlee (the college is searching for a Kootenai elder to work with Kootenai students). Although Arlee is a fluent Salish speaker, language instruction is only one part of the program. Students also learn the traditional activities of the Salish people throughout the four seasons.

In the fall, for example, students learn about hunting and preparing and sorting game. In the spring, the focus turns to gathering roots and other wild foods. Arlee also presents the songs and spiritual aspects of these and other seasonal activities. Although one formal, on-campus language course in Salish grammar is included, most time is spent off-campus. As a result, language is learned informally, but also more naturally, crossing what Finley said is an artificial boundary between language and culture.

Other colleges participating in the Learning Lodge Program share this philosophy. Although each tribal college has devised its own unique approach, all emphasize the importance of elders and traditional knowledge.

On the Blackfeet reservation, the Learning Lodge Institute supports a summer immersion camp. Participants begin their studies on the Blackfeet Community College campus, learning the fundamentals of the language. Then instruction is moved to an isolated campsite, a place so remote, said Marvin Weatherwax, that it can only be reached by horses and four-wheel drive vehicles. Students and instructors live together in tipis, haul water, and go without electricity for a week. "They live, eat, sleep, and learn at the site for a week of intensive language and cultural instruction," he said.

The program asks a lot of students, but Weatherwax said 250 to 300 people participate annually. The immersion camp is only one piece of a larger, reservation-wide effort to teach language. An additional 200 students are introduced to the language through courses taught in the college. Meanwhile, children are now learning Blackfeet in Head Start programs.

Tribal colleges are given the freedom to devise their own programs. Indeed, this emphasis on local control is central to the Learning Lodge effort and to the larger Kellogg initiative. But the Learning Lodge Institute also encourages colleges to share what they have learned. A newsletter is published, programs are being recorded on video, and a gathering of faculty and students is organized annually. Inspiration for their work also comes from Hawaii. In 1998, Lanny Real Bird visited language immersion schools at all levels—from pre-K to grade 12—on the Island of Hawaii where "no English" was the rule.

Linking Language and Culture

What, ultimately, do the colleges hope to achieve? The immediate goal is to build community support for language survival, devise promising teaching methods, and begin teaching a new generation of tribal members. Even one new fluent speaker is, then, a sign of success. But, beyond these immediate and measurable outcomes, Learning Lodge participants believe language is essential for the survival of tribal cultures.

Lanny Real Bird summarized the goal this way: "Without a language to speak, there is no culture because there are words and expressions unique to particular tribes. They are holy and supernatural. To be translated and used in the context of interpretation of another language . . . would not be possible."

Marvin Weatherwax gave an example from everyday experience. "I can tell somebody something in English, and it will sound so plain. Maybe I would say, 'Would you give me a glass of water?'" But in Blackfeet the same request translates this way: "'Would you please take me to the water?'"

"It has such a different feeling when you say it this way," he said. "Each word and phrase has spiritual connotations."

So the loss of language is more than the loss of words. Instead, "it would be the loss of culture as it is," Weatherwax concludes. "I cannot teach you culture. Culture is something you have to live. Through the language we can give a part of the culture that can be lived."

Paul Boyer, PhD, is the founding editor of the Tribal College Journal.

Rekindling the Anishnabe Language Fires at Bay Mills

By Jennifer Dale

Anishnaabemowin—speaking the Anishnabe tongue—is a skill many Anishnabeg have lost. But the language fires were never entirely extinguished, and now Bay Mills Community College fans the flames with its Nishnaabemowin Language Instructors' Institute. Five years after the institute was established, many Anishnabeg people are coming to see the institute as the path for regaining the language, which others refer to as Ojibwe or Chippewa.

The only language program of its kind in Michigan, the instructors' institute is a landmark for Bay Mills and the region. The Nishnaabemowin Language Instructors' Institute consists of three summer sessions, and the first class graduated last year. Not only do the students benefit, but the communities are also benefiting, according to Doris Boissoneau, who developed the language institute curriculum. After learning enough language fluency and traditional teaching skills for classroom teaching, graduates take their knowledge home as a valuable resource to their communities. The students come from all over Michigan, Canada, Minnesota, and Wisconsin. From young adults to grandparents, the students represent 15 different tribes in the Great Lakes region. Our people have finally gotten the opportunity to go to a place to relearn, regain, and retain *Anishnabeimadziwin* (life), said Boissoncau.

This venture by Bay Mills Indian Community is a tremendous task, and we are just beginning to see the rewards. The third-year students are beginning to converse and understand the language, said Barb Nolan, one of three course instructors.

For decades, the Anishnabe community strove to keep the Ojibwe language from disappearing. Despite boarding schools' efforts to eradicate the language, elders retained it and taught it in the communities. Alice Fox wrote lessons for the Johnson

"Rekindling the Anishnabe Language Fires at Bay Mills" appeared in *Tribal College: Journal of American Indian Higher Education, 11*(3), in spring 2000.

O'Malley Program. Frank Hugo taught children of Bay Mills Indian Community. But Fox and Hugo passed away, and most others of their generation are following. "Our elders are leaving, and the next generation are not speakers," said Boissoneau.

Early History of Language Efforts

Before the institute was established in 1994, language instructors had no support, and those who wanted to learn found it very difficult. With English as a first language, it would be easier to learn the closely related German language than an unrelated language like Ojibwe. "There were no curriculum programs, no resources, no teachers, no school," Boissoneau said. Others taught classes over the years, but no effort imparted the fluency necessary to preserve the nuances of Ojibwe. Everyone knew a few words— *Ahneen* and *Miigwetch,* how to introduce themselves, the names of their clans, and a few other words here and there.

In the community, opinions varied about the importance of regaining the language. Some Anishnabeg wondered if it really was that important: they had survived as a people and that was enough. Other elders took the opposite point of view. They said that those who cannot speak their own language are only people whose ancestors were Anishnabe; they are no longer Anishnabe themselves. "It's harsh, but I kind of agree with that view," said Tom Peters, who graduated from the institute this year. Peters views the Anishnabe language as a sacred gift. "Language is a first step to recovering culture. It's authentic culture because the Native perspective is not taken out of it." His fellow graduate, Sidney Martin, agrees. "The language means everything. It is the pow wow, the culture, the basket making, the values," she said. "It is everything." Boissoneau said, "If we are going to call ourselves a Nation with sovereignty rights and inherited rights, we need a language and a culture."

The efforts of these early teachers were not in vain; they preserved the people's enthusiasm and desire to learn more. Boissoneau entered the picture in 1996 after the tribal college offered her a free hand to develop a curriculum for its summer language institute program. A full-time instructor at Sault College in Sault Ste. Marie, Ontario, Boissoneau agreed to spend her summers in Michigan at the institute.

Her Native language is precious to Boissoneau, who is a member of the Wikimikong First Nation in Manitoulin Island, Ontario. When she was only six, Boissoneau was taken to a boarding school 120 miles from home where she suffered physical and emotional abuse. Despite her ordeal, she managed to hold on to her language. In 1996, Boissoneau received a language teaching degree from Lakehead University, Thunder Bay, Ontario, Canada. In October, Ontario Lieutenant Governor Hilary Weston presented her with the Order of Ontario, the highest recognition from the provincial government. It was presented to honor the impact she has had on her Ojibwe language students, who nominated her. "My mother gave the language to me freely; she didn't charge me. I'm giving back the gift I got."

Holistic Curriculum

Boissoneau has developed a holistic curriculum for the summer institute that is Anishnabe-driven, taught by Anishnabe faculty. Language is incorporated into all the classroom experiences. Over four years, students develop their proficiency so that by the time they graduate, they are equipped with language abilities, teaching skills, and can incorporate cultural components. "They are being given skills to teach basic Ojibwe in any public school," said Boissoneau.

Each new summer session starts with a pipe ceremony and talking circle. Students and instructors talk of their journeys and the purpose that brought them to the institute. The program runs for six weeks and is equivalent to a college semester. Although the summer session ends in July, students continue to receive year-around instruction and support through fall, winter, and spring immersions. Boissoneau credits the students for going through a grueling study of the language, much more intense than a university program.

The instructors' institute is always evolving. At first, third-year students stayed with a Wikimikong family in Canada for a week of total immersion. The students found the families to be too quiet among strangers, however, so the next class of third-year students practiced total immersion on-site with a number of fluent speakers. Boissoneau's graduates are now working on a one-of-a-kind language manual—30 lesson plans in which language, structure, and orthography are developed by Anishnabe speakers, incorporating English later. "It will give instructors a starting point," she said. Next year's graduating class will also work on instruction materials.

Boissoneau's prediction that the graduates would benefit their communities seems to be coming true. Graduates teach Ojibwe across the state at both K-12 schools and colleges. One graduate, Tom Peters, has developed computer language learning games for tribal schools and is working on an Internet Native radio project. He and another graduate, Ted Holappa, have received the Frank Victor Hugo Memorial Award, established in 1998. Hugo worked on language preservation in the 1970s and 1980s until his death in 1993 after a long struggle with Parkinson's disease. His example and memory help keep the Anishnabe language and culture alive.

"The fires have never gone out amongst the Anishnabeg," said Boissoneau. "They have dimmed. The adults and elders are rekindling the fires, and they will burn even brighter and rekindle the hopes of all Anishnabeg."

Jennifer Dale is the editor of Bay Mills News, *a Native newspaper serving the Bay Mills Indian Community located on the Michigan shores of Lake Superior.*

Using Blackfoot Language to Rediscover Who We Are

By Duane Mistaken Chief Sr.

Niitsitapi is translated as real people. In order to be that, you have to be real and true to who you are. Too many times, culturally relevant material is created by simply adding on "cultural components" to the present curriculum. There is no real effort to work from the base of the tribe's philosophy, ideals, and language. In fact, some of the "culturally relevant" material is not culturally specific but merely pan-Indian. Pan-Indian material is a real problem.

If we are going to talk about and implement a Niitsitapi-specific curriculum and philosophy, it darn well better be just that—Niitsitapi. Our elders and grandparents have expressed their concern about misrepresenting our way of life and giving out wrong information by saying repeatedly, *Minniiksistapipohtok Kiipaitapiisinnooni* (don't take our way of life in the wrong direction). But it is a tough struggle to maintain the integrity of our way of life when we teach it to others, especially when our people's minds have been colonized for such a long time.

This is why the Red Crow Community College is establishing the Niitsi-tapi Teacher Education Project. The project is a joint effort with the education faculty at the University of Lethbridge in Alberta, Canada. The program is aimed at addressing the Blackfoot people's concerns about education philosophy, curriculum, and cultural relevancy.

The teacher education project will consist of a four-year Bachelor of Education and a post-graduate diploma that reflect the cultural underpinnings of the Blackfoot Indian communities of southern Alberta and northern Montana. The project relies heavily on the use of the Blackfoot language and other cultural components. Project planners hope to graduate teachers who understand Blackfoot epistemology, pedagogy, and ideology. The project will also enable teachers to develop strategies and

---

"Using Blackfoot Language to Rediscover Who We Are" appeared in *Tribal College: Journal of American Indian Higher Education, 11*(3), in spring 2000.

techniques for applying these concepts in the classroom. As a result, students will have a better understanding of their cultural heritage and identity.

Understanding Values

As the curriculum is being developed, Red Crow Community College and the university have proceeded with professional development courses to assist teachers who are presently teaching in schools on the Blood and Peigan reserves. The program has introduced a uniquely innovative approach designed to reach the project's cultural goals. In the fall and winter of 1998-99, we developed and conducted two courses.

The first course was *Kiipaitapiisinnoon*, Blackfoot Culture as a Living Experience. The course objectives were to develop an understanding of the Blackfoot values of *Aina'kowa* (respect), *Isspommotsiisinni* (sharing), *Kimma-piipitsinni* (kindness), and *Atsimoihkanni* (good heart). The course was also intended to relate these concepts to the students' and teachers' everyday lives and to the classrooms.

The instruction team included Betty Bastien, PhD; Cathy Campbell, PhD; Johnel P. Tailfeather, MEd; Pete Standing Alone, Horns Society and Ceremonial Grandfather; and myself, Duane Mistaken Chief, researcher and present member of the Horns Society. The participants were the teachers from neighboring schools.

Between each class, participants were asked to talk to the elders and grandfathers from any of the four Blackfoot reserves in southern Alberta and northern Montana. We make a distinction between elders and grandparents. An Elder is any person with a great deal of knowledge and experience, who is also of advanced age. *Naahsinaniksi*—our grandparents—are former members of the sacred societies who are two generations separated from the present members of those societies, just as in the family structure. Age is not a determinant.

The participants in the class then discussed their findings in a talking circle with instructors. The grandfather would elaborate on any items that needed clarification. The classes were very emotional at times, and courses were interspersed with tears and laughter. Many participants explained that they cried with happiness as they realized how rich our heritage is.

The teachers gathered for these professional development classes for three hours on seven Friday afternoons. Each class commenced with a prayer by the grandfather in attendance—Pete Standing Alone. In the words of an elder, "*Atsimoihskaani Isstohkoipommikapi Kiipaitapiisinnooni* (prayer is what has brought all the good in our lives)."

Following the prayer, I would begin the class by breaking down the word or concept of the week and explain how the various parts of the words relate to other terms in our language, our spirituality, values, philosophy, etc. This gave the participants a more in-depth understanding of not only the words and concepts but also about who they are as Niitsitapi individuals. The class then took turns in a talking circle discussing what they had found out for themselves as they had researched the assigned words and concepts. Participants were also required to keep a journal reflecting on the new knowledge, their findings, and how they could implement that knowledge in their lives. Throughout each session the grandparent would answer any questions related to the sacred. The instruction team answered other questions.

The most unique part of the course was that it was conducted almost entirely in the Blackfoot language. During the planning stages, Dr. Betty Bastien said the course had to be conducted in Blackfoot because the value of the research and instruction would be lost in translation. "The language is alive," she said. "When we translate it to English, we lose that life."

Going into these courses, we didn't know how successful they would be. We certainly did a lot of praying for guidance. Enthusiastic reviews from the first group of participants led to a second course, which enjoyed just as much success as the first one. Leo Fox, principal of the Lavern School on the Blood Reserve wrote his response in the Kainai board of education newsletter. He said he learned with the help of elders how to better understand concepts that he assumed he knew before. He learned to apply

Ainna'kowa (to show respect) to himself, saying, "*Ainna'kohsit!*" (respect yourself). "By knowing ourselves better, we should have more empathy and understanding about the people we work for," he wrote.

Our Language Speaks to Us

Dr. Betty Bastien and I believe that in order for Blackfoot people to heal ourselves, we must return to who we are as Niitsitapi. We must regain our identity so that we can truly choose what direction to take in our personal lives, whether it is mainstream or Niitsitapi. At the present time, our education systems are almost identical to the mainstream, and therefore we are merely being taught to fit into the dominant society. We don't have a choice. We must deconstruct our colonized thinking. Coming to know who we are goes a long way toward this deconstruction.

Our research has helped us realize that the language is a very important source of philosophical knowledge. The language holds much of what we need to know about ourselves. I learned that as I researched words and phrases. Those phrases came from a way of life and philosophy that even our own people have said is lost. It isn't lost. It is here, and much of it is in our language.

I am personally very pleased that we used the Blackfoot language as the source of re-discovering our philosophies and knowledge. Our language speaks to us and reveals to us our philosophies. We just have to start listening again.

Duane Mistaken Chief Sr. is the cooperative education coordinator at Red Crow Community College.

Little Priest Tribal College Immerses Students in Language

"Just as it was with our relatives long ago, we must continue to keep our language alive so we can pass it on to future generations," Isaac Caramony intoned in fluent and lyric Ho-Chunk (Winnebago). His student audience sat in rapt attention as he spoke of the importance of the Ho-Chunk language immersion class he was helping to teach. The students had just undergone three weeks of complex drills in a subject most were novices in, yet they were eager for more. Little Priest Tribal College's (LPTC's) language and culture program sponsored the three-week, summer language immersion class.

"Attendance at LPTC Ho-Chunk classes is increasing due to the successes of past and current students. When one student demonstrates increased Ho-Chunk language proficiency, that inspires others to do the same," language program coordinator Elaine Rice said. Last November, the students began a six month series of classes, one weekend a month at the college in Winnebago, Nebraska. Since the class focuses on using Ho-Chunk in the home, adult students attend for six hours on Saturday and bring their children to the three-hour Sunday session. The classes are given in Ho-Chunk with no other language spoken, allowing students to hear and become comfortable with the sound of the language. No notes or other written materials are allowed during class time, requiring students to learn through practice and memory. After each weekend session, however, families take pre-printed notes and pre-recorded audio tapes home to sharpen their Ho-Chunk skills.

Zena Reeves, LPTC Ho-Chunk instructor, and Rice decided to introduce the language immersion concept to local students while it is still feasible. Rice said, "Figuratively speaking, the language waters are still ten feet deep so we can immerse ourselves in the resources we have. In a few years, if we do nothing, our fluency—our resources—may be too shallow to allow us to have these classes."

"Little Priest Immerses Students in Language" appeared in *Tribal College: Journal of American Indian Higher Education, 11*(3), in spring 2000.

Is language important to sustain a culture and the identity of a tribe? Many others in the Winnebago community believe so. Lorelei DeCora, director of the Winnebago Diabetes Project, told the class that the sessions are part of a holistic approach to improving the physical and mental health of the people. "The language connects us to every other aspect of our life as tribal members," she said. "But you also have to think about learning with reverence. That's the essence of what our Ho-Chunk language is about."

Giving Voice to Crow Country
The Crow Place Name Project

By Carrie Moran McCleary

Interstate 90 follows the Little Big Horn River north from the Wyoming border through the Crow Indian Reservation in Montana. The 2.2 million-acre reservation is nearly twice as big as the state of Delaware, but it is filled with mountains and grasslands, not pavement. Except for the interstate and an occasional powerline, the rolling grasslands offer few reminders of the 21st century. It is easy to imagine the Custer and Reno cavalry forces on the hilltops with their Crow scouts. From the Little Big Horn valley, the Wolf Mountains are visible 30 miles away. On the west side of the reservation near the Pryor Mountains, one can still follow the ruts of the Bozeman Trail while watching the deer and coyote wander in the coulees. Horses graze amongst the cottonwoods in downtown Crow Agency (the reservation's capital city), often with children clinging to their backs.

Except for one green sign stating, "Now leaving the Crow Indian Reservation," most people never realize they are in Crow country at all as they drive down the interstate. With the exception of the occasional historic marker and the Little Big Horn Battlefield itself, visitors do not realize the rich, living history of the area. Few could imagine that Little Big Horn College (LBHC) is using sophisticated technology to preserve that history.

From the car window, visitors see signs saying "Rest Stop" and "Mission Creek." There are no signs for *Anmaalapammúua* (Where the Whole Camp Mourned), *Baáhpalohkahpe* (The Place where the Crows first Celebrated the 4th of July), and *Bisshíilannuusaau* (Where They Laid Down Yellow Blankets). Travelers won't know the rest stop between Hardin and Billings is known as Anmaalapammúua because a war party that fought at Rainy Buttes in North Dakota returned with many dead in 1864.

"Giving Voice to Crow Country: The Crow Place Name Project" appeared in *Tribal College: Journal of American Indian Higher Education, 12*(2), in winter 2000.

It is said that so many warriors were killed, not one family went unaffected.

Most visitors won't realize the spot between Reed Point and Big Timber was once a favorite camping site of Crows. It is also where the Crows celebrated the Fourth of July for the first time. The Burlington Northern Railroad sponsored the celebration in 1882 and brought in Crows who were camped at Absarokee, Montana, on flatbed cars. The railroad workers named a child born during the celebration George Washington, and that child became the tribal leader George Washington Hogan.

The area known on Euro-American maps as Mission Creek was the site of the first distribution of annuities to the Crows after the treaty of 1868. Part of the annuity included yellow army blankets, and to this day many Crows call the area Bisshíilannuusaau.

None of the English names for these places say much about their history. Even for the younger generation of Crows, the journey from Crow Agency to Bozeman might be marked by the amount of gas money needed for the trip and by remembering where so and so's apartment is—"You know the place we stayed that one time on the way to the powwow."

Chronicling Stories

For Phenocia Bauerle, however, the 200-mile drive has become a living history because of the stories told by her grandfather, Dr. Barney Old Coyote. A Crow tribal member and decorated World War II veteran, Old Coyote is a humble man who possesses vast knowledge about his tribe's culture and language. Now retired, he has spent his entire adulthood passing that knowledge on to his children, grandchildren, and the next generation of Crow people, as well as students at Montana State University and LBHC.

Over the past two years, he and almost 20 other Crow elders have worked with LBHC general studies instructor Timothy McCleary to document Crow place names across Montana and to chronicle the many stories behind them. Their Crow place names list now boasts over 500 locations from the reservation and other places that Crow people historically visited across North America.

Old Coyote came to our home on a sultry July evening to talk about the project. He brought his grown daughter, Jackie Old Coyote, and sat with a cup of coffee in his hands, his graying hair slicked back. He told us about Crow names for far-away places like the Crow's Nest in Canada, the big woods in Minnesota, and even the Arkansas River: "They [the Crow] didn't like to go beyond the Crow's Nest [in Canada] because they heard it was poor country; too cold, poor animals, and bad heat."

As Old Coyote related his stories, Jackie listened intently. She has undoubtedly heard the stories before, but she must have been committing them to memory again. The tall, slender, young woman, a screenwriter, actress, and model, lives on the reservation and commutes to Los Angeles for her work. None of her father's words were lost to her, and she was concerned that he seemed uncomfortable in the heat.

Crow place names refer to physical characteristics, such as a creek with a fork or a place to gather wild carrots. This can lead to repetition. For example, in the weeks before the annual Crow Fair, people will say they are going to *Aliiliiluttuua* to gather teepee poles. If the speaker is from the Pryor district of the reservation, the listener knows where he is going in the Pryor Mountains. If a person from the Black Lodge District says the same thing, he is most assuredly referring to a location in the Big Horn Mountains, Old Coyote told us. The "Chief of all Shade" (*Alaatchiawacheeitche*) can be found in both the Big Horn and Lodge Grass districts.

Old Coyote is fully aware his non-Indian neighbors lack awareness of the culture that surrounds them. Euro-American maps of his reservation and of Montana show place names that do not mean much to the Crow people, places such as *Iichíilxaxxish* (Spotted Horse Creek), which Old Coyote pronounces with the hard double X guttural sound rolling out from the back of his throat. He explains: "Spotted Horse had become a great leader and chief among the Crow. He was such a great man that he was well respected even by his enemies. And yet over the loss of a horse to his little brother in a horse race, he lost his temper. He beat his little brother to a pulp, so from then on in [the ways of] Crow culture, there was no respect for him because he had beaten a little one, so far beneath his stature. This happened at Spotted Horse Creek." Old Coyote's non-Indian neighbors call the same place "Sunday Creek," leaving no meaning or lesson in Crow etiquette for the 8,000 Crows still residing on their reservation.

Old Coyote says that in some cases English translations of Crow names corrupt them. "One thing I noticed is White people like colorful names of how they think of Indians, and they often don't match what they are," he says. For example, he mentions a place in Billings, Montana, called *Aashuúchoosalaho* (Where there are Many Skulls). "White people call it Valley of Skulls, which gives the impression of human skulls," he says. To the Crows, however, the number of skulls indicates abundance of game, because you didn't take skulls with you when you butchered a buffalo. So what non-Indians think of as a graveyard, many Crows consider a place of prosperity. He refers to his children and grandchildren often, and he has told them many stories about the Creator, Old Man Coyote, and place names. "Maybe they won't remember them all, but they will know some."

As Old Coyote talks, McCleary eagerly listens, taking notes, looking at maps, hoping to glean more information. Every time he talks with Old Coyote, he learns something new about Crow culture, world views, or language.

Although McCleary is a non-Indian, he has worked at the Crow community college for the past 10 years. He is now a competent Crow speaker, much of which he owes to language classes taken from Old Coyote. With his training as an anthropologist McCleary is constantly on the outside looking into the Crow world. Because of his long tenure here, however, this light-faced, red-headed man is considered by many to be a part of the Crow community. This gives him the unique opportunity to see things that others might take for granted. McCleary weaves this cultural knowledge into the curriculum at the college. In 1997, McCleary published a book on Crow star knowledge, which is used in classrooms across the reservation, including an astronomy class at the college. Both Old

Coyote and his brother, the late Mickey Old Coyote, contributed to the book.

McCleary says the place-name project information can be incorporated into the college's Montana history class, Crow history class, and Global Information Systems (GIS) class, as well in Crow language classes. Bilingual instructors utilize the information to introduce language, history, and culture into the classroom.

Old Coyote says the project keeps the place names among the Crow who he feels are losing their Crow language skills and history. "I like to see the project progress," Old Coyote says. "It gives hope for the future that we will not lose our Crow identity. When something is already in print [Euro-American maps] it is hard to change. This can correct those distortions of the past," he adds. "I see LBHC as becoming a clearinghouse as well as a depository of this information."

Evolution of the Project

A historic and battle sites tour given by the tribal college in the summer of 1991 gave birth to the place name project. When McCleary watched videos of the bus tour, he was immediately struck by the multitude of stories told by the four elders, Barney Old Coyote, Phil Beaumont, Joe Medicine Crow, and the late Mickey Old Coyote. The elders had so many stories to tell that they could not complete the story for one location before the bus was passing another site with cultural significance for the Crow people.

"They had descriptions of almost every little point and drainage as they traveled," he says. "They didn't always know the dates of events, like a Euro-history professor would, but they knew incredible details about what took place there. It became apparent to me that where it took place and what occurred are more important to the Crow people."

McCleary says the project has confirmed some beliefs about Crow culture and brought him a better understanding. When Crow people name something after a historical incident, it is usually an extraordinary event, he says. "Nearly two-thirds of the Crow place names are references to the way the land looks or the directions a stream flows, unlike Euro-American names which are named after people or events," McCleary says. As examples of topographic names, he mentions *Baa'hpakuhke* (Short Butte) and *Alasa'htapumme* (Small Coulee). "This tells me the Crow see themselves as equal to the land and do not try to dominate it."

Last summer, McCleary received funding from the Learning Lodge Institute at LBHC (an initiative supported by the Kellogg Foundation) to interview more elders and record their information. The results from all of the interviews are now available on a database linked to the college's website. The database contains GIS maps of each location and can be accessed by the English or Crow name, and by reservation district. McCleary trained bilingual teachers from across the reservation on how to access the site over the summer. LBHC chief information officer Randy Falls Down created the website and supervised student Collins Gaurdipee, who created the computer-based maps.

Falls Down said the project's potential for classroom use is important. "For a bilingual teacher to just look out the window and point at something and say its name in Crow makes it more interesting for students. Kids love their computers," he says. "With this, they can connect their culture into it. It's just a good deal all the way around."

Carrie Moran McCleary is a member of the Little Shell Band of Chippewa who grew up in Washington and Montana and works on the Crow reservation.

Back from the Brink
Innovative Language Program at Fort Belknap College Involves Three Generations

By Ron Selden

Fort Belknap College[1] has embarked on an ambitious project in Montana to pull the Gros Ventre and the Assiniboine languages back from the brink. Government relocation programs, boarding schools, Christian indoctrination, and other forms of assimilation have combined to endanger many Indigenous languages across the country. On the Fort Belknap Indian Reservation, where there are two principal tribes, only a handful of Gros Ventre, or White Clay, members are still fluent in the traditional tongue. The number of Assiniboine, or Nakoda, speakers is a bit higher.

The tribal college already offered classes in both the White Clay and Nakoda languages as part of the school's general curriculum. In 2002, they started the Speaking White Clay Project, a mentorship program that matches eight Gros Ventre elders with eight young adults. However, college officials realized they needed to reach children. "There is scientific evidence that when children learn their Native language, they have a higher self-esteem. And when people feel good about themselves, this enhances everything they do," Lynette Chandler of the college explains. "Studies also show learning a Native language optimizes children's learning capabilities. It strengthens their ability to symbolize and conceptualize and enhances their cognitive learning abilities, which applies to all areas of study—reading, writing, math, and science."

The Speaking White Clay Project included plans for youngsters in 2005, but Chandler became impatient. She is a Gros Ventre tribal member who recently earned her master's in Native American studies. Despite the lack of funds for the younger

---

[1] Fort Belknap College changed its name to Aaniiih Nakoda College in 2012.

"Back from the Brink: Innovative Language Program Involves Three Generations" appeared in *Tribal College: Journal of American Indian Higher Education, 15*(4), in spring 2004.

students, she and others, including her husband, Sean Chandler (also Gros Ventre), launched a fledgling after-school program. The college supplies classroom space and allows her to take time from her other duties to direct the Speaking White Clay Project. A small group of preschool and elementary students comes to the college five days a week and speaks only White Clay for an hour a day.

The students mainly learn their ancestors' tongue through a method known as "total physical response," which involves learning through action. They also learn prayers and traditional songs. Various games, such as bingo, have been translated into White Clay. The students, teachers, and tribal elders work together to create new words for modern items.

The young adult instructors for the after school program are learning their language skills as they go through a mentorship program, which is funded by a three-year, federal Administration for Native Americans grant. Each of the eight apprentices works with a fluent Gros Ventre elder. The elders—Elmer Main, Theresa Walker Lame Bull, Moses Nez Perce, Merle Skinner, Dorothy Kinsey, Joe Iron Man, Fred Gone, and Leona Bell—serve as the masters. The apprentices are working toward state certification in language instruction.

The college plans to incorporate the Nakoda language, which is well established in college coursework, into the curriculum as soon as possible. Eventually they hope their apprentices will be teaching language to all ages, from Head Start through 12th grade.

Chandler figures that money will follow success. Comments from the after-school participants indicate that the tribal members' dedication runs deep. Student Jenessa Talks Different says, "The White people made the Indian people stop speaking their language because they said it was bad. We're doing this because we want to learn." Lynette and Sean Chandler's oldest daughter, Shondlyn, who is six, is in her second year of language classes. She's already teaching her infant sister a few Native words each day.

"I really feel like our language is alive. It's just dormant right now," Lynette Chandler says. "It's alive within our elders, and it's alive in our children. The community is very supportive of what we're doing. I think that comes from the elders. They're so proud."

Ron Selden was a freelance writer and photographer based in Helena, Montana.

Teasing Aside
Little Big Horn College Maintains Crow Language and Culture

By Luella Brien

Chartered in 1980, Little Big Horn College (LBHC) is dedicated to the preservation of the Crow language and culture. "It was mandated from our ancestors that we continue to do that," says Dr. David Yarlott, president of LBHC.

Crow Language instructor Alden Big Man adds, "The language makes us who we are." One Crow language class and two Crow culture classes are part of the general requirements for graduation. Crow Studies offerings include Crow Social and Familial Kinship, Crow language I and II, Conversational Crow, and others. These courses give LBHC its own unique identity as a college, Yarlott says.

The kinship class, one of the most popular classes offered, outlines the different social and family relationships in the Crow culture and discusses the different acceptable behaviors within those relationships. "Students want to know about relationships between people," Yarlott says, "not only about blood relatives but clan relationships and society relationships." Working families have disrupted the traditional means of passing on this kind of knowledge. "It's only done superficially in most families now." The weakening cultural links between family members cause most students to take the cultural courses to rebuild those connections.

The Crow language classes also fill up quickly. Grammar, syntax, and basic vocabulary are covered in Crow I, while Crow II builds on the basics. Conversational Crow, which covers terms and phrases used in everyday conversations, has only been offered for a few years, but speaking Crow is becoming popular again, Yarlott says. "It's going against the old trend of thinking that to be successful, you had to speak only English," he says.

"Teasing Aside: LBHC Maintains Crow Language, Culture" appeared in *Tribal College: Journal of American Indian Higher Education, 18*(2), in winter 2006.

Big Man welcomes the new trend. He took over the language classes last spring and hopes to create a safe environment for students to learn the language. "Like learning any language it takes repetition. We give them the tools," he says. "But there are some who don't speak it because they are shunned or ridiculed due to our social and familial kinship that conditions us to tease everyone."

The Crow clan system has teasing clans. Each Crow child is born into his or her mother's clan and father's clan. The father's clan is the teasing clan. Teasing clans are designed to tease children to make sure they don't grow up too arrogant or undisciplined. In recent times, however, teasing has gone beyond clan responsibility. People now tease in everyday interactions, regardless of clan affiliation. Big Man believes students would practice using the language without fear of ridicule if teasing were set aside at the college.

The college is comprised of 85 to 90% Crow students, 10 to 15% non-Crows, and a handful of non-Native students, Yarlott says. Nearly three-fourths of the students speak Crow as their first language, but the number of Crow speakers decreases each year. Most of the faculty, staff, and administrators speak Crow, and many are LBHC grads. "In order for us to excite our young people they must have role models who have gone through the same process," Yarlott says.

Close to 80% of the graduates transfer to four-year institutions to pursue higher degrees. In May 2006, 41 students graduated with associate's degrees, including two students who graduated with an Associate of Arts in Crow Studies.

Luella N. Brien (Crow) is a reporter for the Ravalli Republic *in Hamilton, Montana.*

Language of the People Forever
Bay Mills Spins Thread Tying Ojibwa Communities Together

By Brenda Austin

Why would anyone want to spend thousands of hours away from home and pay hundreds of dollars in tuition to acquire one of the world's most difficult languages? For Anishinaabe people, that is an easy question to answer. The Ojibwa language is the thread that ties communities together and unites all Anishinaabe as one people sharing a common culture.

Ojibwa (also known as Anishinaabe or Chippewa) people live around the world. There are over 30 distinct tribal entities or reservations of Ojibwa living throughout their original homelands in the northern United States (Michigan, Wisconsin, Minnesota, North Dakota, and Montana) and about the same number of First Nations in southern Canada (Ontario, Manitoba, and Saskatchewan).

Bay Mills Community College (BMCC) serves its Ojibwa community in the Upper Peninsula of Michigan, offering classes based in tribal culture, similar to what other tribally controlled colleges do. However, it has found an important niche for itself through its 6-year Ojibwa language immersion program, which is unique in the world.

The *Nishnaabemwin Pane* Immersion Program translates into English to mean "language of the Nishinaabe forever." The director, Ted Holappa (Keweenaw Bay Band of Chippewa), says language students always should ask whether their program eventually creates a speaker of the language. For the Pane program, the answer is yes.

"We offer students 100% immersion into the Ojibwa language. Language is not learned, it is acquired. 'Learn' is a term implying conscious learning whereas when a language is 'acquired,' it is done in the same way a toddler acquires language, by being

"Language of the People Forever: Bay Mills Spins Thread Tying Ojibwa Communities Together" appeared in *Tribal College: Journal of American Indian Higher Education, 19*(3), in spring 2008.

immersed in it and listening to it. Nobody gave us grammar books in English when we were toddlers," Holappa says.

According to Holappa, most language students entering the Pane program have never heard Ojibwa spoken by a fluent speaker. "Language acquisition is unconscious learning that exposes students first to hearing the language, then to listening to the language, to begin to understand what their instructors are saying."

The program's associate director and principal instructor is Barbara Ann Nolan, who is a Ketegaunseebee Anishinaabe from Garden River First Nation in Ontario, Canada. She says, "You have to listen to a fluent speaker in the language for 2,000 hours, and you will then understand about 95% of what that person is saying. After 6,000 hours of being totally immersed in the language, you are functionally bilingual. At 12,000 hours, you would be a fluent speaker. It's a long journey that depends on the individuals and how motivated and committed they are."

Prior to creating the Pane program, BMCC offered a Nishnaabemwin Language Instructor's Institute lasting three summers for six weeks each summer. Most students who attended the summer instructor institute were not speakers of the language and did not come out of the program speaking the language. They learned some basic grammar and culture and spent the last 12 weeks of the course developing a portfolio and curriculum to take into a classroom to be used to teach Ojibwa grammar. The students developed course work for use by both non-speakers and fluent speakers of the language.

Evolution of an Inspiration

Holappa says, "I was one of those individuals who had taken every language course offered locally and in Sault Ste. Marie, Ontario, Canada. After about 10 years of studying the language, I got so proficient in grammar that I developed three grammar courses, which I then taught at BMCC.

"But I still couldn't understand what a fluent speaker was saying to me, let alone engage in a conversation beyond the basics.

I was very frustrated and wondered if maybe I wasn't working hard enough, or maybe I wasn't smart enough; heaven forbid that maybe my teachers were not good enough. I asked myself why I couldn't speak this language that I had worked so hard at and understood so well," Holappa says.

"I began meeting others who were equally frustrated, like John Paul 'JP' Montano (Pokagon Potawatomi) and Wanda Peron (Keweenaw Bay Band of Chippewa) among others. We decided there had to be another way of acquiring the language. Almost every language student enters a language program not to conjugate a verb but because they want to speak and understand the language. But the instructors were teaching us the language the way they were taught. They were taught by linguists, and linguists teach the structure of a language."

Holappa, Montano, and a few others volunteered to research how people acquire languages. "Learning grammar methodology to my knowledge has never produced a speaker," Holappa says. "We discovered the acquisition mode of teaching language during our research into how the Maori, Hawaiians, and French Canadians were so successful in teaching and retaining their languages."

Through the guidance of Holappa and Montano, today's Pane program has come a long way since the first summer instructor institute. After about three years of volunteer work and research for BMCC, Holappa and Montano asked Barb Nolan to teach an immersion class. "When we had our first immersion class and the instructor spoke in the language for about an hour, it hit me that was the most Ojibwa I had heard in the past 10 years of my studies," Holappa says.

"I had heard words but never in the context of talking about subject matter. That class went over so well that we added a second class, and we are now into our 5th year," he says. That first class evolved into BMCC's six-year, full time program, 12-14 credits every semester. Next year the tribal college may celebrate the first graduating class of about 20 students completing the six-year program.

Ojibwa is a complex language. To translate one Ojibwa verb, Montano and the team needed over 640 pages for all of the conjugations, and the language has 25,000 plus verbs. "You can't memorize this language word by word. You have to be here immersed in the program where the language is washing over you," Holappa says.

Kathy LeBlanc (Keweenaw Bay Band of Chippewa), language student and teacher of Native American studies, says, "If our language falls apart, it wouldn't be long before the rest of the community and culture follow. Then you are just part of mainstream America, and why have a reservation if you don't even know what tribe you are? What makes us special is our language and culture."

Ojibwa is one of the hardest languages in the world to acquire not because it is hard to pronounce but because it is so descriptive. Ojibwa is about 80% verbs as compared to English, which is about 80% nouns. "The language can express almost anything in a wide variety of beautiful melodic ways," Holappa says.

"For example, the word for depression in Ojibwa is *nibodendam*, meaning the feelings of a dead heart. When you listen to a fluent speaker talking about something or praying in the language, your heart just soars if you understand it. Much of our culture and who we are as Anishinaabe is transmitted through the language; that is why it is so important to maintain and pass on this language," Holappa says.

Every Minute Counts

Barb Nolan has been teaching Ojibwa for the past five years. She grew up speaking the language. "I feel funny when I speak English," she says. "I even quit speaking English at home and to students at school. Every minute counts; every little minute of language acquisition fills their language acquisition device. Even when I see students at the store or on the reservation, I speak to them in the language," she says.

Nolan says she looks at helping students acquire the language as her second chance. "I didn't speak the language to my own kids all the time as they were growing up." While studying for her master's degree, she learned that her children could have grown up bilingual if she had spoken to them in Ojibwa only while her husband spoke to them in English. "You can't change the past, but I have been given another chance to pass it on to my students," she says.

Holappa says, "I am old enough that I can see the progression of identity. I know old Indians who we would consider very traditional who don't even realize they are Indians. They are just living their life. There are other Indians who put on the trappings of an Indian: Identity is not just wearing Indian clothes or putting on the cultural artifacts of a tribe but knowing who you are, where you came from, and who you belong to.

"That kind of identity is much stronger and concrete than external symbolic expressions of being an Indian. The college through language programming and awareness classes is expending energy to get that sense of identity inside of ourselves and our students," he says.

Between the programs offered off campus and at BMCC, the Pane program now has over 100 enrolled students acquiring their Native language. Holappa says, "This little community college is doing something very unique in terms of culture and language. There is now a real strong sense of hope in the college and community that in fact the language has the possibility of being passed on and preserved, where before I didn't think it did."

Brenda Austin (Sault Ste. Marie Tribe of Chippewa Indians) has been a writer and a photographer for her tribe's newspaper, Win Awenen Nisitotung.

Firing Up White Clay
Immersion School Students Encouraged to Return, Give Back

By Kurt Umbhau

Fort Belknap College[1] president, Carole Falcon-Chandler, does not fluently speak the *A'ani* (White Clay) language, but her granddaughter does. The girl, one of the 12 students in the White Clay Language Immersion School located on the college campus in Harlem, Montana, is part of the next generation of fluent A'ani speakers.

The language immersion school keeps the same group of students, or cohort, until each student reaches high school. The students are from ages 9 to 12, in grades fifth through seventh. Soon, the 12 students will transfer to different high schools, but when it is time for college, Falcon-Chandler hopes the students enroll at Fort Belknap College.

Falcon-Chandler notes the difference between her boarding school education and the scene unfolding outside her campus office: "White Clay wasn't encouraged. That is why many people from my generation don't speak the language." She chuckles at the past, revealing, "Back then, I even belonged to a square dancing club."

The children learn traditional games, she says, and as they play, they speak and shout in A'ani. "I'm looking out my window over at the language school; they have a great big playground," she says. "We do everything we can to accommodate those students because they are such an important part of us."

In contrast, during her own boarding school education, Native language was not part of the curriculum. Throughout the 19th and 20th centuries, the federal government forced assimilation by exterminating languages. In 1880, the Indian Bureau issued

---

[1] Fort Belknap College changed its name to Aaniiih Nakoda College in 2012.

"Firing Up White Clay: Immersion School Students Encouraged to Return, Give Back" appeared in *Tribal College: Journal of American Indian Higher Education, 21*(2), in winter 2009.

regulations for agents stating: "All instruction [for Indians] must be in English ...and the conversation of and communication between the pupils and with the teachers must be, as far as practicable, in English."

A century later, the Native American Languages Act of 1990 recognized that such federal policies "often resulted in acts of suppression and extermination of Native American languages and cultures." Now under the law, it is the policy of the United States to encourage and support Native American language survival and educational opportunity.

When White Clay was outlawed, some members of the tribe, also known as the Gros Ventre, kept the language alive. One of the elders who helped maintain the language was Theresa Walker Lamebull. She passed away in 2007 at the age of 111.

In a 2002, Lamebull recounted that when caught speaking White Clay at a mission school, the teachers "made us kneel in the corner for a couple of hours…I learned a lesson." Nevertheless, she organized a language group and kept speaking A'ani, hoping to ultimately pass the language on like a beacon from one generation to the next.

White Clay Language Immersion School director, Lynette Stein-Chandler, an enrolled White Clay Indian, hopes to recover the nearly lost language. Today, students are instructed in A'ani as well as learning cultural games, tribal values, and academic skills. "We are training the next generation of A'ani speakers, and we are hoping to grow our own teachers through the immersion school," she says.

The school uses the partial immersion method, in which instructional time is divided equally between English and A'ani. However, Stein-Chandler emphasizes that they embed cultural teachings when subjects such as math and reading are taught in English. "We understand the importance of education," she says. "We give our students every tool we can so that they will be successful in their educational endeavors, but we constantly stress our mission is to produce fluent White Clay speakers."

Stein-Chandler is the catalyst behind the language school's success and growth. When she began the program in 2002 as a graduate student at Montana State University, White Clay was almost extinct, with just eight fluent speakers. Since then, the school has blossomed from an after school class to the leader in tribal college language immersion programs.

Falcon-Chandler confirms that the immersion school has rapidly become an integral part of the college. "Nationally, we are recognized as the leader in the Native American immersion schools on tribal college campuses," she says. "We were the first, and we now are consulted on how to develop programs at other tribal colleges, and it is all because of one person's dream and then a lot of support."

Under Stein-Chandler's leadership, the program has also received government funding, facilities, college assistance, and community support. Last year, the federal Administration for Native Americans (ANA) gave the program the ANA Commissioner's Award for outstanding success.

Another key factor to the White Clay linguistic revival is Sean Chandler. Chandler is the primary A'ani language teacher, and he is also the departmental head of Native American studies at Fort Belknap College. A White Clay Native, Chandler devotes much of his time to teaching language and culture to the immersion students. "We don't pay him," says the director. "He just does that to help us."

But many Native languages remain in jeopardy of extinction. According to the 2009 Senate testimony of Linda Taylor of the American Indian Higher Education Consortium, of the 155 indigenous languages still being spoken in the United States, 135 or more are spoken only by elders.

At the White Clay Immersion School, educators are also developing college-level language courses and a certificate program with the Montana Office of Public Instruction. Lynette Stein-Chandler emphasizes the well-rounded education that the students receive. They are preparing students to compete academically but also instilling within them a sense of responsibility to the White Clay Tribe. "They are obligated to speak A'ani to their children. And this philosophy of returning and giving back is part of our core values," she says. "Each of our students is taught that in lessons and by example. These values are embedded in them."

Carole Falcon-Chandler notes that immersion school students will have opportunities to teach White Clay in the future: "It is important that our college students take traditional languages. To earn their first degree, they are required to take a course in the language. So if we have some of our own immersion school students [who] make it back to teach the college-level courses, we will have seen the full circle and will have so much personal pride for taking a nearly lost language and preserving it."

"Our students aren't going to be successful unless they are proud of who they are," she adds. "Our tribal college students are inspired to see not just the A'ani language reclaimed, but to have lively young students on the campus getting both a modern and traditional education." Language is "the heart of who we are," says Falcon-Chandler. "Language is part of us, and it is important that we don't lose this vehicle of transmitting our culture."

Kurt Umbhau, MA, was editor of Tribal College Journal, *2009–2010.*

Ojibwemotaadidaa
Preparing a New Generation of Fluent Speakers

By Persia Erdrich

Upon hearing the intermittent, explosive laughter emanating from the classroom, the casual passerby may think a comedy writing class is in session. But this is serious business. The laughing students are part of an intensive language immersion program and are trying to learn Ojibwe, one brain-bending verb conjugation at a time. Perhaps it is odd that revitalizing a language is at times laugh-aloud funny, but participants in this program learn Ojibwe through all sorts of media, including, stories, jokes, skits, and games.

Ojibwemotaadidaa Omaa Gidakiiminaang (let's speak Ojibwe to one another here on our Earth) is an Ojibwe language immersion program funded by Fond du Lac Tribal and Community College (FDLTCC) and with grants from the State of Minnesota. Robert "Sonny" Peacock, director/CEO of FDLTCC; Dr. Gary Deason, a retired professor and writer; and Lucia Bonacci, a recent graduate of the Ojibwe language program at the University of Minnesota, Twin Cities (UMN) conceived the program at Camp Ottertail, an Ojibwe language and culture camp in Ontario, Canada.

With a development team that included FDLTCC president Larry Anderson, among others, participants sought to create a program where students could learn Ojibwe at an advanced level. At that time, students who had graduated from other Ojibwe language programs and hoped to continue their studies had to do so on their own. Even though a growing demand for Ojibwe language teachers created jobs for these graduates, they did not have an organized program where they could increase their own fluency.

The development team decided that an advanced Ojibwe language program should be conducted completely in Ojibwe—

"Ojibwemotaadidaa: Preparing a New Generation of Fluent Speakers" appeared in *Tribal College: Journal of American Indian Higher Education,* 24(4), in summer 2013.

only a true language immersion setting could produce highly proficient to fluent speakers. These Ojibwe language learners could then go on to contribute to other language revitalization efforts at the preschool, elementary, and college levels.

The development team employed multiple first language speakers from different Ojibwe communities to give varied examples and applications of the language. The immersion program would have a student to first speaker ratio of one to one, if possible. This would increase the students' time with first language speakers and allow for individualized teaching and learning. It would also give students the opportunity to hear people interact with one another in Ojibwe. Speakers could work together and discuss the intricacies of the language and teaching techniques with one another, modeling the usage of the language for students to hear and mimic.

The Ojibwemotaadidaa immersion program has two parts. The first is a three-week Ojibwe immersion academy scheduled during the summer at FDLTCC. Elders, students, and staff stay at the college dorms and meet each day at the college's Anishinaabe Waaka'igan (Ojibwe House). This facility is complete with classrooms, bathrooms, a kitchen, and a comfortable living space. It is somewhat isolated from the rest of the campus, which allows the participants to speak Ojibwe at all times. Participants also spend time in the forest around the campus and have access to the Ojibwe Resource Center along with the college's recording studio. Students and elders are in close proximity every day for extended periods of time. The setting helps to build personal and professional relationships amongst the participants. As of last year, students could earn six academic credits for participating in the three-week academy.

The second part of the Ojibwemotaadidaa immersion program is a series of Ojibwe immersion weekends offered once a month during the school year at the Cloquet Forestry Center. This facility, located near FDLTCC, is a conference space with classrooms, a dormitory, and miles of trails through the woods. These weekends provide an immersion opportunity for students who cannot commit to the three-week Ojibwe immersion academy.

A variety of first speakers come each weekend so that students can learn about the diversity of the language and those who speak it. During the day there is a multitude of activities with first speakers, both inside college facilities and in the surrounding forest. In the evenings, Dr. Brendan Fairbanks from UMN teaches Ojibwe grammar and learning strategies. These immersion weekends offer a unique opportunity for teachers to directly apply what they have learned over the weekend to their own classrooms.

Complete immersion allows students to use Ojibwe in many different contexts and situations. Students hear and participate in conversations in Ojibwe that might not occur in other learning environments. They talk about shopping or plant medicines, hear jokes, and, most importantly, they engage in everyday interpersonal communication. A trip to the grocery store or a cribbage tournament generates new vocabulary. The Ojibwemotaadidaa program emphasizes how the language can be employed in everyday life, not merely for certain situations, conversation topics, or as a subject of detached academic interest.

Complete immersion is also highly intense. For this reason, there is a rigorous application process, which requires an essay in Ojibwe as well as a video of the student speaking the language. Applicants must prove that they are committed language learners who can withstand the pressure of an Ojibwe-only environment. And it is pressure! Complete immersion results in wild gestures, stick figure drawings, and desperate faces. Nobody can use English. Brendan Fairbanks tells new students, "Sometimes you just have to make a fool of yourself to be a successful language learner." English is literally checked at the door. Students must surrender cell phones, computers, iPods, and any other devices that would expose them to English. Sometimes this hurts—but it works. Students are immersed so completely in the language that they begin to think in Ojibwe.

By creating a network of language learners and first speakers who have successfully worked together under intense immersion conditions, the Ojibwemotaadidaa program has helped revitalize the Ojibwe language by permeating families, communities, and classrooms. Language assessments conducted by UMN have found that students significantly improve in their speaking and comprehension over the course of the three-week academy and the immersion weekends. Students with the least language fluency coming into the program showed the most dramatic improvement. And students with more advanced language skills were able to attain higher fluency in the language. This is especially important for Ojibwe language teachers who are on their own as skilled speakers in their classrooms. By speaking with elders, they can practice and learn how to teach the language more effectively.

The Ojibwemotaadidaa program at Fond du Lac Tribal and Community College has been successful because language learning is not purely academic. Tribal colleges and universities are the ideal venue for such programs, as they are institutions where cultural life, spirituality, humor, and learning intersect. FDLTCC's program emphasizes that the fluent first speakers of the language are the experts. And by bringing fluent speakers and language learners together, the integrity and diversity of the language is ensured.

In the fall of 2012, the second Ojibwe immersion weekend program started, and this summer will mark the third year for the three-week Ojibwe immersion academy. Over the past three years the Ojibwemotaadidaa program has continued to grow and thrive. When asked about his involvement in creating the program, Robert "Sonny" Peacock explained, "There is a power and beauty in learning your language, there is a joyousness about this group learning it, and it stays with you when you go out the door. At the end of the day I get a sense of satisfaction by having been a part of it. It's a good feeling."

Persia Erdrich (Turtle Mountain Chippewa) is the program coordinator of Ojibwemotaadidaa, an Ojibwe language immersion program at Fond du Lac Tribal and Community College.

Louis Soop and Language Restoration at Red Crow Community College

By Mary Weasel Fat

Louis Soop is a Blackfoot language instructor at Red Crow Community College (RCCC) located on the Blood/Kainai Reserve in southern Alberta, Canada. He is a fluent Blackfoot speaker and has been teaching the language for 20 years. A traditional singer, dancer, and actor, Soop is a member of the RCCC Eminent Scholar Program, which was established to recognize elders who possess spiritual and cultural knowledge and who utilize their knowledge in various programs at Red Crow.

Soop belongs to the sacred Horn Society, a religious/spiritual society of the Blood Tribe Sundance. Although he holds both Bachelor of Arts and Bachelor of Science degrees from the University of Lethbridge, Soop credits the sacred Horn Society for his Blackfoot language and spiritual knowledge. It is one of two religious societies on the Blood Reserve: The Horn Society consists of three members for each bundle—a man, his wife, and a male partner; while the Motokis Society is the Buffalo Women's society.

"My knowledge of teaching comes from the Horn Society where members learn all about the Blackfoot language, culture, ceremony and songs," he says. Soop is passionate about teaching the language: "It's important we know our language, also to know various sounds and spelling of our language. . . . I teach it so they [his students] will know the different sounds and how to pronounce them."

Soop explains that Blackfoot uses only 12 letters from the English alphabet and one sign, called a glottal stop, which divides a word into two parts. "Before you can teach the language you need a methodology of teaching. You can't use big words with 20 letters," he says. He starts with greetings, weather reports, days of the week, months, dates, seasons, colors, and numbers. And "you

"Louis Soop and Language Restoration at Red Crow Community College" appeared in *Tribal College: Journal of American Indian Higher Education*, 24(4), in summer 2013.

have to know the difference between past, present, and future," he adds. Sometimes the class uses the *Blackfoot Dictionary of Stems, Roots, and Affixes* by Donald G. Frantz and Norma Jean Russell, but most of the time it's not needed. He also employs Blackfoot language symposiums, which are hosted alternately by the four Blackfoot tribes—Blood/Kainai, Piikani/North Peigan, Siksika, and Aamsskaapipikani/South Peigan (or the Blackfeet Tribe of Montana). RCCC hosts this symposium, as does Blackfeet Community College across the border in Browning, Montana. The language is spoken at the symposiums, and participants discuss ways of transmitting it to their respective tribes. Although the four Blackfoot-speaking tribes have their own dialects, they understand each other.

Soop often begins his courses with an orientation so that students will know what to expect of the language. He devises lessons on reading and writing, uses films like *Circle of the Sun*, and invites members of the RCCC Elders Advisory Council to make cultural presentations. Students do a research project pertaining to the culture and take both midterm and final exams. He also assigns a family tree exercise. "It's important you know who your relatives are," he maintains. He often takes students on field trips to museums such as the Provincial Museum in Edmonton, the Glenbow Museum and Archives in Calgary, the Galt Museum and Archives in Lethbridge, and the Siksika Museum in Siksika, Alberta.

In teaching the Blackfoot language at RCCC, Soop has various resources at his disposal. The Kainai Studies Department—which also employs language instructors Duane Mistaken Chief, Ryan Heavy Head, and Narcisse Blood—utilizes a website that has its own Blackfoot phraseology and stories applications devised by Blood Tribe elders. The Blackfoot Digital Library also has Blackfoot stories and other resources that RCCC students can access, while the RCCC Resource Centre's First Nations Information Connection portal provides access to the Blackfoot dictionary. The portal offers free online resources which are shared with the other six tribal colleges in Alberta.

Although such modern technology can facilitate learning, Blackfoot incorporates traditional values, Soop states. Blackfoot ceremonies consist of language and song, about half and half. He feels that there is more interest in speaking the language when people join Blackfoot social or religious societies, believing people want to pray and speak in their own language. If you know the language, Soop maintains, you know your culture because culture is imbedded in language.

Mary Weasel Fat (Blackfoot) is the library coordinator for Red Crow Community College.

Blackfeet Community College Develops Montana's First Language App

By blending the future of technology with the history of tribal language, Blackfeet Community College (BCC) has developed Montana's first Native American language application for smartphone users. The BCC Blackfeet Culture and Language Division has been working on the first phase of the "app" for nearly six months. The division teamed up with Ogoki Learning and developed the first of many apps for the Blackfeet language. The free app is available to Apple iPhone users. The Android version will be available later in 2013.

BCC president, Billie Jo Kipp, stated, "We are pleased with the innovation that division chair Mike LaFromboise has initiated in the development of this app. BCC is poised to be first in the advanced technological development of the Blackfeet Language. This type of ingenuity represents the many talents that BCC has to offer and a melding of our history to the future of technology."

The application is a quick and easy reference guide to numbers, phrases, colors, and more. The goal of the project's first phase was to establish an avenue to teach the tribe's younger generation a few words or phrases. "We feel we can connect all generations by using communication tools that the younger generation prefers. We offer a cultural teaching opportunity utilizing cutting-edge technology," LaFromboise stated. He went on to note that the college was working on future upgrades for Phase I based on feedback from the community. The Blackfeet Culture and Language Division has also initiated plans for Phase II of the project and hopes to include Blackfeet bands in Canada.

"BCC Develops Montana's First Native Language App" appeared in *Tribal College: Journal of American Indian Higher Education, 24*(4), in summer 2013.

Iḷisaġvik College Offers Language Nest Program

By Devin P. Bates

Iḷisaġvik College's language nest program, Uqautchim Uglua, initiated a new Iñupiaq early learning Associate of Arts degree to meet the college's goal of increasing the number of Indigenous certified teachers on Alaska's North Slope. This degree offers a holistic approach with a traditional Iñupiaq emphasis, and is designed to support Native students in their learning experiences while meeting accreditation requirements. A strong Iñupiaq studies component has been incorporated into the degree program with 12 required credit hours of Iñupiaq language and cultural and traditional arts. Students can choose from an education or business track. The degree will prepare students to open their own language nests, become educational paraprofessionals, or continue their education at a four-year institution to become certified teachers.

The first cohort was launched during the spring 2013 semester, as Uqautchim Uglua brought students together for a brief residency at Iḷisaġvik College. Courses are offered via distance education to facilitate the participation of students living in the outlying villages across Alaska.

An Iñupiaq language immersion nest and teacher training center also opened at Iḷisaġvik College this past November. Early learning practicums are conducted in Iñupiaq for up to 12 children, ranging from birth to three years of age.

Besides the early immersion program, students' parents participate in a parent empowerment group and interview elders to capture traditional parenting information. The information gleaned will be compiled and shared with partnering institutions and language nests. Traditional parenting information will also inform the college's education courses.

"Iḷisaġvik College Offers Language Nest Program" appeared in *Tribal College: Journal of American Indian Higher Education, 24*(4), in summer 2013.

Due to these efforts, there has been progress in embedding the Iñupiaq culture and values into the college's early learning Associate of Arts program. College president Pearl Brower states, "Iḷisaġvik College is Alaska's only tribal college. Part of our mission is to perpetuate our Iñupiaq culture, language, values, and traditions. The creation of the Iñupiaq early learning degree and the start of the language nest movement on the North Slope fall directly into the mission of the college."

Uqautchim Uglua is one central embodiment of a serious, consolidated, and sustained effort by the people, communities, and entities of the North Slope to Indigenize regional education systems, increase the number of state-certified Iñupiaq teachers on the North Slope, address issues pertaining to child care, and attack Native language and culture degradation concerns head on.

The project is supported by a grant from the American Indian College Fund's Wakanjea Sacred Little Ones project, which is funded by the W.K. Kellogg Foundation, the Alaska Native Education Program, the North Slope Borough's mayor office, and Iḷisaġvik College.

Devin P. Bates served as the director of the Uqautchim Uglua language nest program at Iḷisaġvik College.

Lakota Documentaries
Working with Cultural Heritage at a Tribal University

By Jurgita Antoine

In this essay, I will discuss the preservation and interpretation of cultural heritage, as well as the economic aspects of such work at Lakota Documentaries project at Sinte Gleska University on the Rosebud reservation in South Dakota. When Don Moccasin (1948-2009) started recording elders on the Rosebud reservation in the 1990s, his goal was to preserve the Lakota language and culture for the future generations. In 2000, his efforts became an elder documentary project now called Lakota Documentaries at Sinte Gleska University. Moccasin videotaped elders and community events to capture the oral tradition, history, cultural knowledge, personal stories and lifeways of the Lakota people. The interviews also document Lakota and the ways it is used by fluent native speakers today.

This work is especially important since Lakota is an endangered language. Survey estimates for Lakota fluent speakers vary from 6 to 14%. In the reservation context, it is more meaningful to talk about extended families and generations within those families who maintain the language. Today, almost all *tiyospayes* on Rosebud have at least one generation (elders) fluent in Lakota. Remote communities such as Spring Creek have families with two fluent generations (elders and adults), in which case the children are still exposed to the language. According to the latest survey conducted by one of the Rosebud Sioux tribal language programs, 77% of respondents indicated that they had at least one fluent speaker in their family. Lakota language still remains an important part of Lakota identity and reservation life, as it is associated with traditional ceremonies and highly respected elders and leaders.

Don Moccasin was a member of the *Aske* tiyospaye (Wrapped Braids extended family) of the Rosebud Sioux tribe. He was an active participant in his culture as a fluent speaker of Lakota,

"Lakota Documentaries: Working with Cultural Heritage at a Tribal University" appeared in *Anthropology News*, March 2014.

teacher, singer, and social and ceremonial dancer. Moccasin visited and recorded elders in reverence to his father, a World War II veteran. His father had wanted to honor the elders by visiting and feeding them, but passed away before doing it. As he was good friends with or related to most of his interviewees, the recordings also capture Lakota communication practices when both conversation participants are familiar with the cultural context of the stories.

In Lakota society, elders are venerated as the source of knowledge and wisdom, and they provide leadership and guidance to their families and communities. In Lakota culture, knowledge is validated through individual experience. Therefore, people with the most experience—elders—are valued most. Also, this individual approach to culture allows a lot of diversity within the culture. As individuals have different experiences, so do their interpretations. Thus, one might hear different interpretations of the same story or song, all of which would be considered valid since they are based on the interpreters' individual experiences and relationships with the culture. Linguist Paul V. Kroskrity (2009) notes that in Native American communities, even dialectal variations exist at the family level. In comparing interviews by elders from different tiyospayes, we found that every Lakota family uses the language differently, including sentence structure, connectives, vocabulary, and metaphors.

Today, the project team continues Moccasin's work in cultural heritage preservation. The project's priority is digitization and translation of recordings. Another important task is the creation of contemporary written Lakota texts based on the transcripts of Moccasin's recordings. We also continue making new recordings and prepare educational materials. Fluent Lakota speakers lead the project team in the interpretation process as they transcribe, translate, and contextualize the stories under the guidance of an elder.

Lakota literacy remains a challenge for the community as the language to this day is mostly oral and many elderly speakers do not use written Lakota. Although Lakota is a relatively well-documented language—dictionaries, grammars, and texts are available—we should not assume that all Lakota speakers know how to read it. Some time ago, as we were searching people who could translate the recordings, I took a text with a video recording to an elder who volunteered to help us. She watched the video and then studied the printed Lakota transcript for a long time. When I finally asked her if she could understand the text, it turned out she did not read Lakota. Later she worked on a team with her daughter, who was transcribing the text and relying on her mother to explain certain words or expressions. Another speaker who was interested in the work also admitted that she did not know how to read or write in Lakota.

Despite that, tribal members thoroughly enjoy interpreting their cultural heritage. Translation work enables them to reestablish the links between the past and the present, and also brings thoughts about the future generations. It changes people's relationship with the culture and language, which for so long has been a cause of discrimination and inequality. It raises the community's interest in the language, as elders call each other to discuss rarely used words or family members share their translation experiences over dinner.

We adopted the mentor-apprentice model, successfully used in endangered language learning for translation work. We noticed that elderly speakers knew the language, but had limited literacy and technology skills. We started pairing them up with a younger relative, who had those skills, yet was not as fluent in the language. Although grant requirements limited our use of this model, the participants enjoyed their work and developed different skills in the process. The elders became more comfortable with technology and Lakota orthography, while the younger participants were learning Lakota language and culture.

Every translator brings his/her own relationship with the language, culture and text. In the mentor-apprentice model, the learner develops these relationships through the elder, who helps him/her understand the language and who also imparts the cultural context of the stories, metaphors, and even certain words. To this day we lack adequate Lakota language curricula and learning materials; this model of studying video recordings and texts with an elder has a lot of potential for language learning.

Since Lakota language is endangered, some educators and outside researchers expect that language and culture documentation work should be welcomed by tribal members who would collaborate for a symbolic fee or no fee at all. However, in a poverty-stricken reservation, where unemployment rages up to 83%, cultural heritage is seen as one of the very last resources of the community which could be used for economic benefit.

Lakota language and traditional cultural practices were maintained in the most marginalized communities on the outskirts of the reservation, away from towns, where poverty rates are the highest. Although Lakota language and traditional knowledge, including stories, songs, and prayers, are still vital to the fabric of the community, they have become specialized knowledge, accessible only to certain individuals or families. In the past, such specialized knowledge was transmitted either in the family or for a fee in a mentor-apprentice type of setting.

Thus people protect their language and culture as an economic resource, which makes documentation efforts difficult. This approach also discourages Lakota literacy as written works grant public access to carefully protected knowledge. Any outside work with Lakota cultural heritage is seen as redirecting resources from the people to whom they belong—the families that have preserved Lakota language and culture. Yet, people do enjoy documenting and interpreting their cultural heritage. Such opportunities are viewed as potential jobs, which will provide them and their families with much needed resources.

Jurgita Antoine, PhD, served as a project director of Lakota Documentaries at Sinte Gleska University.

References

Hinton, L. (2001). The Master-Apprentice Language Learning Program. In L. Hinton & K. Hale (Eds.), *The Green Book of Language Revitalization in Practice* (pp. 217–226). San Diego: Academic Press.

Kroskrity, P.V. (2009). Embodying the Reversal of Language Shift: Agency, Incorporation, and Language Ideological Change in the Western Mono Community of Central California. In P.V. Kroskrity and M. Field (Eds.) *Native American Language Ideologies: Beliefs, Practices, and Struggles in Indian Country* (pp. 190-210). Tucson: University of Arizona Press.

A Rebirth for the Lakota Language
Institute Hopes to Create a New Generation of Speakers

By Christopher Vondracek

Dawn Frank breaks from the interview to answer a family text message. Her daughters attend Stanford University. When they text back home to their mom and aunts on the Pine Ridge Indian Reservation in South Dakota, it's often in Lakota. "We're just sharing logistics on a family event," says Frank, vice president for instruction at Oglala Lakota College in Kyle. "Here," she points to the final expression, laughing, "They're just asking if there'll be coffee."

Lakota, once suppressed by the boarding school system, is on the rise in western South Dakota. For the first time, the Lakota Language Consortium (LLC) hosted a two-week Lakota Summer Institute on Pine Ridge, one of the parcels of land allotted to the western bands of the Sioux in southwestern South Dakota.

The two-week summer institute in Kyle came from Frank's determination to get professional development for her faculty. "It's about speaking," she says, over a lunch of beef stew, blueberry soup, fry bread and fruit punch, as students and teachers intermingled during the lunch hour in the foray of the Lakota Language Immersion School on the Oglala Lakota College campus.

"Alex," she calls to a teacher passing by, "How much did you know?"

"Only phrases here and there, mostly from ceremonies and songs," says Alex Firethunder-Loeb.

Now, Firethunder-Loeb, 28, is a teacher. And he hopes that his students will grow in their language, too. "To have all these people here in my home, across the road from me, it's just a lot of positivity and empowerment."

For 11 years, the Lakota Summer Institute has been housed at Sitting Bull College in Fort Yates, North Dakota, on the Standing Rock Indian Reservation. Organized by the Lakota Language

"A Rebirth for the Lakota Language: Institute Hopes to Create a New Generation of Speakers" appeared in *The Rapid City Journal*, June 18, 2018.

Consortium, an organization formed in 2004 by Lakota community members and linguists based in Bloomington, Indiana, who work to revitalize the language, the institute comprises classes teaching not only the language but how to teach the language too.

Lakota was never written down prior to missionaries and early tribal scholars introducing grammars and dictionaries. The goal of the Lakota Institute, however, is not to teach a book language, but a spoken language. Today, first-language speakers number roughly 2,000. And learning can be costly. "We are the generation who knows what loss is like," says Frank. "I speak, I understand, but I'm like one of the ones who isn't fluent."

Ben Black Bear, 72, who grew up speaking Lakota almost exclusively until the age of 20, led the Lakota Studies Department at Sinte Gleska University on the Rosebud Indian Reservation. On June 7, he led a classroom of fluent speakers who are learning the mechanics of a language they already know. "They still need to learn the grammar and the sound system," he says. "They need to learn how to teach the language."

In another class on June 7, around 20 or so students stood in head linguist Jan Ullrich's class, holding toy animals and asking each other their names. With notecards in Lakota scribbled on the tables, textbooks open, bottles of water or pop out. Joseph Catches, 57, looked on, as a classmate said "big cat"—"*Igmú tȟáŋka.*"

"I'm supposed to be fluent," one student says. "But there were a number of animals I didn't know. I guess only the common ones."

The institute has four classes: three at intermediary levels and one advanced session. Just shy of 80 students completed the two-week program—a remarkable success, Frank says, in their first year. Lunch was provided daily, and each morning two vans went on routes picking people up. Some students came from university in Montreal or as close as down the road in Kyle. Textbooks were free. The goal is to make the language accessible to anyone who is interested.

"Lakota has such an expansive inventory of sounds," says Arman Murphy, an intern with LLC and a linguistics major at the University of Pennsylvania who was visiting South Dakota for the first time. He became interested in Lakota after taking a Native American languages course in the spring. "Compared to many Indigenous languages," Murphy says, "Lakota is very robust."

The orthography developed by LLC's team of linguists is new for some older speakers. Older versions did not include diacritics, for example. The newer alphabet also includes nearly 40 "letters."

Students standing in the lobby after lunch try out what they've learned. "*Khíyotaka yo*," says Otto Cuny, 29, from Martin, which translates as "go sit at the table."

"My grandmother spoke it, but I didn't take the time to get to know it." He now believes teaching Lakota is "kind of like my calling."

His classmate, Destiny Leftwich, 26, earned a teaching degree from the University of South Dakota, where she also took Lakota. But her experience here has been more immersive. "When he talked about revitalizing the language, it was really emotional," says Leftwich. "I want my children to be first-generation speakers."

After lunch in his grammar class, Firethunder-Loeb wears a stiff-brimmed black hat and joshes with students, trying to keep the mood alert during a dry discussion of gendered endings. He works to make the students laugh as they reach the 2:15 p.m. break. Firethunder-Loeb grew up in New York City, but made visits to the reservation during summers to see his mother and participate in cultural experiences. Five years ago, he moved to Kyle and graduated from Oglala Lakota College, but even now, he says, it's rare to hear Lakota spoken on the reservation outside ceremonies and prayer. "It can be heard if you go visit the grandmas and grandpas at the post office. They have a senior citizen's lunch and breakfast, and they'll speak (in Lakota)."

He says it's his goal to break the language out of the classroom. "When I go visit my mom I try to speak Lakota to her. When I talk to my friends who I know are learning, I try to speak it," Firethunder-Loeb says, mentioning he makes posts on Facebook and Snapchat in Lakota, too. Reclaiming language is a small, but important, way to regain a part of culture torn away by assimilation. But the first step is learning the language basics.

At the opening to Ullrich's class, he invites them to share reflections on their learning this week. One student says she's gained a new understanding for how the loss of language can impact political sovereignty. Ullrich nods his head, but redirects the conversation. "This is true, but we must stay focused on the language. We can talk about those things after class."

Then he writes on the board, "*Ečhúŋwičhakhiyapi*," which means "they're allowed to do it." And the afternoon class picks up.

Christopher Vondracek is the education reporter for the Rapid City Journal.

RESEARCH

In the spring of 2004, the American Indian College Fund published a comprehensive, 93-page report entitled, "Native American Language Immersion: Innovative Native Education for Children and Families." Longtime tribal college educator, leader, and scholar Janine Pease (Crow) authored the study, which was funded by the W.K. Kellogg Foundation. It was the first report of its kind, and it offers a detailed look at the state of language immersion programming at tribal colleges and beyond at the beginning of the millennium.[1]

In her report, Pease investigates Maori and Native Hawaiian immersion schools, showing how they have developed new strategies that have been remarkably successful. She argues for incorporating some of these strategies into the immersion programs that were developing at tribal colleges and other Native-serving schools. Further, Pease maintains that through immersion, and language revitalization in general, culture itself, particularly Native ways of knowing and Indigenous knowledge systems, are inherently conveyed to the next generation. In this respect, language revitalization is cultural regeneration.

Pease's study makes a variety of other salient points that extend beyond immersion curriculum and program development. Her research not only illuminates the tremendous advantages that language immersion can have on tribal communities, as it offers the best venue to fluency, but it also buoys Native students' overall academic performance and can help restore familial and community welfare. "The vitality of the language ties directly to the vitality and well-being of the people," Pease writes.

---

[1] Pease abridged this study for the article, "New Voices, Ancient Words: Language Immersion Produces Fluent Speakers, Stronger Personal and Cultural Identities," which appeared in *Tribal College: Journal of American Indian Higher Education, 15*(4), in the spring of 2004. That article also appears in this volume on page 3.

"Immersion improves overall educational achievement, strengthens family ties, and increases retention rates, keeping Native students in school who might otherwise drop out."

Native American Language Immersion
Innovative Native Education for Children and Families

By Janine Pease

Introduction

Native American language immersion schools and projects are the focus of this study commissioned by the American Indian College Fund. The W.K. Kellogg Foundation supported this analysis, to describe and analyze this innovative Native education for children and families. A people's initiative, Native American language immersion encompasses educational practices and social development that lie outside the mainstream language teaching, education, and socialization methods of American children. Native American language immersion programs are characterized by Native ways of knowing, learning, and Indigenous knowledge. Native American organizers demonstrate a profound faith in the traditional Native grandparents' role and their methods in language development, teaching, and learning. Curriculum content and context rely on the rich Native American knowledge bases and their eminent scholars—tribal elders and tribal land resources. Language immersion activists and educators share two characteristics in common: fluency in the tribal language and an unstoppable commitment and devotion to language preservation among children and youth.

Native language immersion schools have remarkable benefits: students show impressive educational achievement, participants demonstrate considerable language knowledge gains in relatively short periods of time, programs contribute significantly to family strength, and college students—adult learners are retained as a positive correlate with language and culture learning. Each of these potentials have importance for tribes, agencies, and organizers (both Native and non-Native) who interact or hope to interact positively and significantly with Native Americans in areas of educational and community development. Creativity and unique qualities characterize the language immersion approaches, and are especially reflective of the tribes and their language.

Native American language immersion is a recent phenomenon in Indigenous tribal communities in the United States. Fifty Native groups are currently engaged in language immersion, planning, and operation. These Native language teaching and learning efforts include year-round schools, summer and seasonal camps, and weekend retreats and seminars. The schools, camps, and programs rely exclusively on the tribal language as the teaching and learning medium. The Navajo community school of Rough Rock, Arizona, has successfully provided their children language immersion for over 20 years. Native family groups and elders have organized Native American language immersion schools among the Blackfeet, Ojibway, and the Assiniboine/Sioux people. Summer and seasonal camps and training seminars have built language understanding for participants of all ages for Northern Cheyenne, Ojibway, and Crow children. Language immersion preschools currently serve several hundred children from the Ojibway, Cree, Assiniboine, and Ute nations. Tribal language commissions and cultural authorities have mandated cultural and language learning that includes leadership training and language teaching and certification. Master/apprenticeship relationships have developed for culture and language learning among the Salish Kootenai of Montana, the Northern Cheyenne of Montana, and the Three Affiliated Tribes of North Dakota: the Mandan, Hidatsa, and Arikara. For Indigenous people, these Native American language immersion activities hold great promise in the areas of education, community, family, and youth development.

Native language educators and activists have taken up the difficult and urgent work of Native language preservation with devotion and commitment. First, there are those who recognize the serious rate of language loss and have made a lifetime commitment to tribal language restoration for the vitality of the tribal nation and its future. Second, Native American children and youth have exhibited stagnant educational achievement (among the poorest achievement of all American ethnic groups). Native language immersion has demonstrated remarkable promise in participants' educational achievement. A third source of motivation to Native language immersion is the greater cultural and language preservation or revitalization effort that strengthens and rebuilds the Native community. Fourth, culture and language teaching and participation positively correlate with Native student retention rates. Fifth, Native leaders foresee a world in urgent need of Native perspectives or worldviews in areas including childrearing, natural resources management, and family and community development. Finally, there are a few activists who are motivated to this work by its political potential to allay the centuries old history of injury and subjugation of Native people. This report analyzes these factors from literature and data. Special emphasis has been given to interviews with language immersion practitioners.

Native language immersion is a practice or methodology of language learning that concentrates on communication, exclusively in the Native language. Total physical response (TPR) is the primary methodology for the Native language immersion classrooms, camps, and projects. Virtually all of the Native language immersion activities are carried out in the context of the tribal or Indigenous culture. Many immersion schools are built and furnished after "gramma's home" and pattern their methods from Native grandparents' ways of knowing and learning. The teachers, educators, and activists have diverse backgrounds; by profession/vocation, they are teachers, bus drivers, retired BIA administrators, Head Start teachers, ranchers, and more. What these educators and activists have in common is a driving, even compelling commitment to language learning and a wellspring of enthusiasm for their students' and participants' potential for speaking and communicating in the tribal language. The students are toddlers and children, middle and high school students, young adults, parents of young children, adults, and elders. Where immersion is happening, all ages of Native people are pursuing the goal of speaking their Native language.

The tribal colleges and universities (TCUs) of this country play a strong, leading role in Native language immersion. These tribal colleges engage their entire community through college student development, community based projects, school-aged educational services, and early childhood education opportunities. The language immersion approaches are especially experiential, and have placed the tribal elders and scholars at the very center of these activities. Through the leadership of the tribal colleges, and in some cases, tribal schools and Indian-owned, non-profit organizations, the cultural experts and Native language speakers provide a Native learning experience. Tribal college students hold a strategic place among the generations of Native people. They are parents of young children, children of elder parents and grandparents, and persons of influence in their communities. Language and culture are at the heart of the TCUs' mission, and now the language immersion activities are moving this mission forward (Stein, 2003, p. 29)

The Native language immersion activities have become a significant part of Native life in over 50 locations across the nation. For these communities, educators and activists have built language learning experiences that are unprecedented in their positive impact on education, individual and family strengthening, intergenerational partnerships, and tribal health and wellbeing. As a relatively new educational phenomenon, it is understood and supported directly by many tribes and their governments, the tribal colleges and universities, and Native-based, non-profit organizations.

While the Native language immersion is young and part of a new genre of culture, language, and educational activity in Indian country, it is not yet a movement. The educators and activists have developed custom designed strategies to deliver Native language immersion. The work of language immersion is demanding and long-term, therefore not "trendy." It's just too hard to do. Activists collaborate locally and occasionally between projects. The commitment required of organizers is immense and time consuming. The implementation demands creativity, expertise, courage, and fortitude. These conditions preclude a "get on the band wagon" potential. Native language immersion is difficult work; work fit only for those few whose devotion to the tribal language, for whatever reason, is unstoppable. This work requires knowing the tribal language and perseverance beyond all measure.

The support for language immersion is problematic. Language immersion costs money, money that most tribal groups can hardly spare in the face of demanding issues in education, health, housing, and natural resources management. Federal funds support language preservation through multiple executive branch-based initiatives.

Most visible is the Department of Health and Human Services, Native language preservation projects. Bilingual education projects in Native languages have only incidentally supported language immersion due to the language transition focus. Private sector support has assisted the development of language immersion and some language immersion schools accept only private funding to avoid the regulations of public funds. Public school funding is highly regulated and therefore nearly inaccessible. The exception is the Diné and Ojibway people who have managed to establish language immersion schools with public school funds. Language immersion funding is a formidable challenge, and a factor that keeps many tribes from this area of education.

Native American language immersion can benefit from the models of the language resurgence among Native Hawaiians and the Maori of New Zealand. During the past two decades, both Native Hawaiian and Maori communities have created and implemented language immersion preschools, schools, and colleges. Indigenous language immersion has made astounding records of educational achievement among the children and youth who participate in language immersion education. The Hawaiian and Maori populations had languished far behind the mainstream educational achievement measures of attendance and completion until the language immersion schools. Language immersion clearly has a role in educational development for Indigenous people.

Principles of Native Language Immersion

Native language immersion principles are derived from interviews with Native American language educators/activists, and from observations of language immersion schools and camps. Literature has been reviewed, authored by practitioners, Indian education scholars, and linguists. These are particularly instructive in the delineation of Native language immersion principles. The practitioner interviews have detailed the methods, strategies, planning, and community support. Teacher qualities and teacher training, parental and elder involvement are delineated. All of these are critical to a Native language immersion school, camp, or project that results in effective language learning and education of Native children and families. Generally, language immersion programs "allow the child or participant to spend part or all of the day learning in the second language. Partial immersion programs operate on the same principle, but only a portion of the curriculum is presented in the second language" (Marcos, 2001, p. 2). Here are the principles of Native American language immersion: Tribal nations' language authorities or commissions officially recognize the urgent and critical nature of their tribal language, its preservation/revitalization, and its relationship to their culture and social wellbeing of the tribe. These tribes have formulated language policies that make the tribal language the official language of the tribe or nation and establish tribal language teacher certification standards (Burnaby, 1996).

Tribal community members and elders who are fluent tribal language speakers work together to plan and initiate awareness activities and introductory language immersion projects as a foundation for language immersion programming. Each project, program, or school is uniquely designed and implemented through this careful, thoughtful, and long-term planning process (R. Littlebear, interview, August 3, 2001).

The design of the Native language immersion schools/camps and programs can best be characterized as intensive culturally based programs. Students learn traditional Native skills, arts, and knowledge, as well as academic subject areas, taught exclusively in the medium of the Native language. Learning environments take the form of "gramma's home" and rely heavily on Native knowledge bases and Native ways of knowing and learning. Camps and retreats are convened in remote traditional encampment sites on tribal lands (W. Wilson, interview, May 11, 2001).

Instructors and resource people in the classroom, schools, and camps share two qualities: (1) extraordinary commitment to tribal language revitalization, and (2) fluency in the tribal language. Tribal elders and cultural leaders are especially integral to the Native language immersion schools and programs, and tribal members are role models related to subject areas (R. Littlebear, interview, August 3, 2001).

The educators/instructors and activists who carry out Native language immersion come from varied backgrounds. Only a few are professional linguists and teachers—most are tribal members with language fluency from all vocational and professional backgrounds.

Language immersion programming is uniquely planned and implemented. The attributes include highly interactive learning, Native traditional hands-on activities, exploration and discovery learning, intense language introduction, and parental and elders mentoring and partnerships.

Master/apprentice and mentor/mentee relationships develop language and cultural leadership. Young Native adults are in long-term learning relationships with tribal cultural elders, to carry traditional knowledge of ceremonies and traditions forward into tribal life. Tribal colleges and universities, chartered by American Indian nations, are responsible for a majority of the Native language immersion programs (Boyer, 1999, p. 12).

A low student/teacher ratio of five or six students to one teacher promotes maximum learning impact. Native language immersion students or participants are all ages. The schools serve predominantly preschool and K-6 children (R. Littlebear, interview, August 3, 2001). Native language immersion funding varies dramatically and is problematic. No generality can be made about sources and methods of funding or resource support. The interviews indicate difficulty in acquiring and sustaining funding (Kipp, 2000, p. 15).

No single description fits the Native language immersion sites. The schools and programs are a Native people's initiative that relies on the millennia-old and tested Native ways of knowing and learning among the generations, and utilizes Native knowledge for content and context. Occasionally, Native language immersion educators/activists associate with one another. Native American language immersion activity in the United States today is recent, innovative, and remarkably reflective of the respective Native identity of the Native people.

Achievement, Language Loss, and Native American Imperatives

National studies on language learning and educational achievement indicate a positive correlation: the more language learning the higher the academic achievement. "Students of foreign languages score statistically higher on standardized tests conducted in English" (Marcos, 2001, p. 1). The 1992 profile of SAT and achievement test takers, published by the College Entrance Examination Board, reported that students who took four or more years of foreign language scored higher on the verbal section of the tests. The Educational Resources Information Center of the U.S. Department of Education has a parent brochure on the benefits of children learning a foreign language. The brochure cites research that shows that second language instruction improves student creativity levels, overall school performance, and gives students superior complex problem solving (Marcos, 2001, p. 1).

As it pertains to students in bilingual classrooms, the development of mother tongue literacy promotes a far better chance of school success (McCarty & Dick, 1996, p. 6). The Northwest Regional Laboratory (a regional agency of the U.S. Department of Education) reported in 1990 that learning more than one language enhances cognitive development, social growth, and promotes understanding among diverse people and cultures (Demmert, 1994, p. 2). Dr. Kenji Hakuta, a nationally known language expert, testified before the National Commission on Civil Rights in 2001 that when the school values and utilizes students' Native language in the curriculum there is increased student self-esteem, less anxiety, and greater self-efficacy (Hakuta, 2001, p. 2). National studies from both the public and private sector emphasize the positive impact of language studies on educational achievement (Sugarman & Howard, 2001, pp. 2-3).

Native language immersion schools and classrooms have existed in several locations for over a decade. Solid data from the Navajo, Blackfeet, and Assiniboine immersion schools experience indicates that language immersion students experience greater success in school, measured by consistent improvement on local and national measures of achievement (McCarty & Dick, 1996, pp. 5-6). Critical educational achievement data exists from the Native Hawaiian language immersion schools in the State of Hawaii. Twenty-two Hawaiian public schools have *Ke Kula Kaiapuni* immersion streams and/or entire schools. In these schools, 1,700 students are enrolled and outperform the average for Native Hawaiian children in Hawaii public schools (Aha Punana, n.d., pp. 6-7). Maori Language Immersion Schools demonstrate astounding educational achievement. Maori student pass rates out of grade 13 (high school equivalent) have hovered between 5% and 15% for decades. Now, with Maori language immersion schools, Maori students' pass rates have soared to 75% (Pease-Pretty On Top, 2002, p. 13).

The language learning carries with it significant forms of satisfaction to the participants themselves, their families, and the elders in the Native communities whose opportunities to communicate in the Native language are expanding (R. Littlebear, interview, August 3, 2001). Youthful language speakers participate in tribal ceremonies and public events, thereby contributing vitality to their communities. Family participation and intergenerational connections are built for a lifetime and create positive networks that build Native communities (Kipp, 2000, p. 14). Native American communities now have operational and meaningful language immersion programs and classrooms, even schools. With varied sources of motivation, language immersion leaders recognize the potentials and benefits of the language immersion experience.

The knowledge of a Native language by Native children, youth, and adults has multiple and important benefits. On an individual basis, Native students develop stronger identities, knowledge of their tribal cultures, and their individual role in and deep appreciation for that culture (Peacock & Day, 1999, p. 3). Language immersion preschool children have developed intense language acquisition, a lifetime benefit in communication (Kipp, 2000, p. 28). For families, the tribal language knowledge holds much of what tribal members need to know about them, for it reveals and teaches tribal philosophies (Mistaken Chief, 1999, p. 27). For the tribal nations, the knowledge of the tribal language is crucial to the combination of factors that build nations, "land, lineage, language, cultures ... a bond born out of respect, the bond links to ancestors as well as to future generations" (Silva, 2000, p. 73).

Darrell Kipp of the Piegan Institute says "language relearning is a journey back home," and details the new and precious bond created between the Piegan Institute preschool children and Blackfeet elders. The Native language clearly embodies a way of seeing, or constructing reality, from a perspective that evolved over many generations. Knowledge of the Native language gives tribal members a unique tool for analyzing and synthesizing the world, and incorporating the knowledge and values of the tribal nation into the world at large (Crawford, 1994, pp. 6-7).

Languages across the world are in crisis. Half of the world's languages are "moribund, spoken only by adults who no longer teach them to the next generation" (Crawford, 1994, p. 1). The language loss among North American Indigenous people is "especially acute," where an estimated 155 languages are still spoken, 210 if you add in the Alaskan Native languages. Of these 135 are moribund; and the U.S. Census of 1990 indicated that one-third of these have fewer than 100 speakers (Crawford, 1994, p. 1).

Clearly, the Native American language usage is declining rapidly in social gatherings, ceremonies, cultural observances, and in the home. Parents are not teaching their children the Native language. "The inability of American Indians and Alaska Natives to speak their language caused many to lose understanding of who they were and what their place was in the universe" (Peacock & Day, 1999). Dr. Richard Littlebear of the Northern Cheyenne tribe, an educator and linguist, says, "The real threat is that too few tribal members appreciate how endangered it (the Northern Cheyenne language) is and have a faith that it can be revived" (Boyer, 2000, p. 13). Native American scholars, tribal officials, educators, and activists articulate the damages wrought on Native American individuals, families, and communities due to the language losses.

Language loss means the loss of linguistic as well as intellectual diversity. Every language loss causes serious damage to individual and group identity, for it destroys a sense of self-worth, limits human potential, and complicates efforts to solve problems in the community. The threat of language death seldom comes to communities of wealth and privilege; rather, language death happens where people need their cultural resources for literal survival. Language death happens to Native American people, the dispossessed and least empowered (Crawford, 1994, p. 7). How does language contribute to survival? Every Native language is replete with symbols of ethnic identity and it is a repository for much of their cultural heritage. The syntax and structure "embodies a way of seeing" the world (Rubin, 1999, p. 1).

The imperatives to save Native American languages are numerous and deliver that urgency with clear rationale. For Native Americans, the rate of language loss is enormous and the cost is immeasurable. Regaining Native American language vitality holds tremendous promise for Native people, for individual, familial, and community strength, and the people's overall wellbeing. For the entire world community, regaining Native American language vitality promises the treasure of intellectual and linguistic diversity. From the models established by the Piegan Institute K-8 schools in Montana, the Native Hawaiian language immersion schools K-12, the Ke Kula

Kaiapuni, and the Maori language immersion schools, the Kohanga Reo and Te Wharekura, the impact on Native American and Indigenous education achievement implies a major imperative.

The Native American community is dramatically undereducated. Language immersion may be the most reliable approach/method and strategy for the acquisition of education.

Education positively correlates with socioeconomic status; the higher the education, the higher the standard of living, health, safety and just about every other index sociologists measure. American Indians are among the fastest growing and youngest ethnic groups in the United States. Altogether, American Indian people make up slightly less than 1% of the nation's population, or 1.8 million American Indian people. The United States government recognizes 510 tribes; another 50 tribes are recognized only by their respective states. Nationally, American Indian people lag behind in high school completion at 61%, compared to 78% for the rest of the American groups. At the higher education level, the under education is more pronounced: 6% of the American Indian adult cohort has completed a four-year degree at the college level, while 28% of the White American adult cohort and 18% of the African American adult cohort has the college degree.

Native Language Immersion, the People's Design

The Native American language immersion activities now number approximately 50 sites. This count comes from correspondence and language immersion educators/activists interviews. The Piegan Institute convened Native language immersion educators and activists in 2000 and 2001 and was attended by representatives from eight sites. The Learning Lodge Institute (a project of Montana's seven tribal colleges) and Northern Arizona University of Flagstaff also assembled language immersion educators and activists.[1] The Indiana University published

---

[1] See Boyer, "Learning Lodge Institute: Montana Colleges Empower Cultures to Save Languages," pp. 94-100.

language revitalization studies authored by tribal language preservation site organizers and teachers. The *Tribal College Journal* devoted an entire issue to language preservation and immersion projects and programs in the tribal colleges and universities. The U.S. Department of Health and Human Services has a division of the Administration for Native Americans, called the Native Language Projects. From these sources, it is estimated that active Native language immersion sites (schools, camps, and retreats) number 50.

Native language immersion schools represent a significant development in tribal language revitalization, cultural preservation, and educational advancement. Only the tribal language is used for teaching and learning in all subjects. Every school has a unique configuration or blend of activities. Language immersion school planning, organization, and implementation requires intense commitment and effort, sustained for many years (Kipp, 2000, p. 20). The strategies and methods used in Native language immersion schools cover a broad range and are reflective of the Native educators/activists implementing the teaching, tribal culture, its oral history and literature, and sciences.

For this study, 10 language immersion schools were reviewed: Akwasasne Survival School (Mohawk of upstate New York), Piegan Institute (Browning, Montana), Lac Courte Orielles Ojibwe Language Immersion Charter School (Hayward, Wisconsin), Southern Ute Language Immersion Preschool (Ignacio, Colorado), Katzebue Public School (Iñupiaq People of Alaska), and Brockton Public Schools Kindergarten and First Grade (Brockton, Montana). Additionally, three schools instruct in a balanced format of Native language and English, two-way immersion, and serve the Diné people: the Rough Rock Community School, the Rock Point School, and the Chinle Public School—select grades.

The Native language immersion schools, camps and activities are a significant development that addresses language revitalization, cultural preservation and educational advancement, concurrently. Teaching and learning in all subjects is conducted only in the tribal language (Rubin, 1999, p. 3). A holistic curriculum is used that is interdisciplinary and without time boundaries (McCarty, 2000, p. 5). The context and content of the curriculum is the tribal culture in its comprehensive knowledge and tradition. This includes seasonal settings in the traditional tribal lands and knowledge bases appropriate to the time of year (W. Wilson, interview, May 11, 2001). Schools have a strict "No English Rule." Language immersion builds fluency in the same learning pattern that an infant learns a first language. The methods rely on a level of fluency that allows the children to think and speak in the Native language, without the delay of translation time. The schools must build sufficient language proficiency, particularly where the students begin school with English as their first language. Based on proficiency, the schools conduct their entire learning environment through the Native language. Generally speaking, the Native language is not a "subject" but the medium through which all subjects are instructed (Kipp, 2000, pp. 29-32).

Teachers (also called instructors, educators, or activists) are tribal members who possess tribal language fluency and the personal stamina to teach and facilitate learning. The educators' common trait is an unwavering commitment to tribal language teaching and learning (R. Littlebear, interview, August 3, 2001). Tribal elders are often the focus of language learning, as they serve as teachers and through their comprehensive cultural knowledge, provide the curriculum content and context (Real Bird, 2000, p. 12). Few teachers are certified by mainstream or state standards, although there are projects that have retained teachers who are also certified in the state systems (M.F. Hermes, interview, October 19, 2001). Many tribal colleges are preparing language immersion teachers, following tribally designated learning experiences; some of these students are also enrolled in a teacher education bachelor's degree program (Stornberger, 2001, p. 2). Searches for language immersion teachers may extend into Canada or across the tribal nations, to locate fluent speakers.

While many methods are utilized in Native American language immersion, three methods have surfaced as key to the schools now in existence. First, the traditional grandparents teaching methods from Native ways of knowing and learning predominates among the schools. Second, the Montessori preschool learning strategies are in use at the Brockton Kindergarten and First Grade in Montana, as well as in the Southern Ute Preschool in Ignacio, Colorado. Third, the total physical response, or TPR, is a methodology for language learning currently in use at the Piegan Institute and the Lac Courte Oreilles Ojibwe Language Immersion School. These three are often combined or blended to make a unique methodology that particularly suits the teacher and students.

The traditional grandparents' teaching methods are predominant, particularly where the tribal elders and fluent tribal members are the primary instructors. The Native ways of knowing and learning follow the household activities and traditional seasonal knowledge areas (W. Wilson, interview, May 11, 2001). This methodology is accessible for most communities, as it consists of the ways in which Native American grandparents have taught their grandchildren for millennia. William Wilson of the Lac Courte Oreilles Ojibwe Language Immersion preschool described this method, "We talk with the children; it is intense interaction . . . we take walks in the woods and all the while, we talk in Ojibwa" (W. Wilson, interview, May 11, 2001).

The Montessori method has been adopted by many Native language immersion preschools, in tandem with the resources to train the instructors and in partnership with a four-year college or university training center tied to this preschool method. Montessori approaches the classroom with interest islands, and follows each child's level of interest. The Native American language immersion schools that utilize Montessori as the delivery method provide the tribal knowledge base and culturally rich learning resources in the "islands of interest." The method does not pre-suppose content or context, and the tribes who have selected this have noted the similarity between this method and "gramma's way of teaching" (C. Baker-Olguin, interview, August 18, 2001). The Southern Ute language immersion preschool is conducted with Montessori methods.

Total physical response is a methodology of progressive learning experiences and language acquisition levels developed with language immersion schools (a center for TPR is located at the University of Minnesota). TPR is useful with "second language teachers, Indigenous language teachers, as it allows students to be active learners, and produces quick results . . . in meaningful contexts" (Cantoni, 1999, p. 54). Strategies include a scaffolding technique that actively demonstrates and builds the learners' receptive language skills. LaFortune describes TPR as a methodology that affords students "the opportunity to recognize fairly sizeable vocabularies useful for early second language acquisition" (LaFortune, 2000, p. 9). Observations of the immersion schools demonstrate the creativity and effectiveness of approaches, especially the Native ways of knowing and learning, a naturally Native approach (R. Littlebear, interview, August 3, 2001). Activists and educators narrate extensive planning and direction throughout the school's existence, with a heavy reliance on a designing committee of advisors and the leadership/stamina of the language instructors (Rubin, 1999, p. 11).

One practitioner describes the Native American language immersion school, "A living experience, centered on the learners with tribal grandparents" (Mistaken Chief, 1999, 26).

The learning experience is approached from tribal perspectives and is highly interactive, and, like a family, is discovery oriented and deals with the student as a whole person (Keami, 2000, p. 52). Immersion schools' curriculum surrounds elders' and instructors' wealth of language and cultural knowledge, and provides experiences, values, protocol, spiritual and traditional philosophical teachings (Real Bird, 2001, p. 12). This combination of elders with children makes an especially powerful learning environment, as it builds significant relationships among generations, and affords cultural immersion along with language immersion (Rubin, 1999, p. 10). Children learn their tribal language in a culturally appropriate content and context, and achieve educational objectives according to national academic standards.

The application of technology to the Native language immersion experience is a topic of great discussion and even controversy. Dr. Richard Littlebear recommended technology as an important supplement to the Native language experience, especially for today's students and their daily interaction with television and computer assisted instruction. Littlebear said that where a tribal language is in critical condition, and the fluent speakers numbers are dwindling, technology is a significant and effective way to apply "life support" to the language learning (R. Littlebear, interview, August 3, 2001).

With advancing technology, there are "unprecedented possibilities" and a basis of hope for aging traditional languages (Rubin, 1999, p. 1). There are language immersion activists who criticize technology as a waste of precious resources, a trade-off for real time and applied teaching and learning directly with children (D. Kipp, personal correspondence, July 6, 2001). The virtue of technology is directly related to the degree of language loss and the stamina or lack of stamina of tribal language speakers. If language loss is severe and the number of elders few, then technology may be the primary resource for Native language teaching and learning, if not the only resource.

Fort Peck Community College (Assiniboine and Sioux Tribes of Poplar, Montana) has Assiniboine and Sioux language learning on-line. The community-at-large has full access to this site for language learning. Indiana University linguist D. Parks has provided important leadership in the development and implementation of computer assisted language learning with the Arikara people at White Shield Schools in North Dakota, as well as at Fort Belknap College[2] in Montana with the Nakoda speakers, and 10 additional tribal groups (Parks, Kushner, Hooper, & Flavin, 1999, p. 3). The Indiana University approach is particularly appropriate to the bilingual education Native language teaching environment, and the integration of language experiences into self-contained elementary classrooms. Native language projects in Canada with the Yinka Dene Institute in

---

[2] Fort Belknap College changed its name to Aaniiih Nakoda College in 2012.

Saskatchewan and the Shimshian People of British Columbia utilize CD-ROM formats that link traditional stories to dictionaries, translations of a story into English, puzzles and games about the story, images and reference materials (Rubin, 1999, p. 8). The Little Big Horn College has an on-line place names site that provides an inventory of 800 historically and culturally significant places on the Crow reservation in Montana.[3] The sites are documented with images, video-clips of the place, and elders recounting the information respective to the site (Real Bird, 2001, p. 3).

Interactive language learning has been happening at Fond du Lac Tribal and Community College in Cloquet, Minnesota, where the master teacher instructs from a central facility to remote locations in middle and high schools in five locations concurrently. The expertise of the Ojibway language scholar can be shared via distance learning technology. Technology has important significance to Native language learning and teaching, and has been successfully applied to immersion schools and camp experiences, as well as language learning within the mainstream school settings.

The traditional Native American methods of learning are well known to Native people. Every tribal nation has a specific set of ways of knowing and learning. For millennia, Native peoples have been self-sufficient in the training of their precious children, youth and adults. They became full and productive members of their families groups and tribal societies. Learning among the people took varied and unique forms, and brought about fine and well-educated tribal members, men and women, who possessed common and special knowledge.

The Native language immersion schools develop literacy in their students at all levels of instruction. Pre-literacy skills are important in the preschools. Teresa McCarty, Navajo language and education scholar, writes about the Navajo immersion schools, "We need to see Navajo literacy in terms of social context,

---

[3] See McCleary, "Giving Voice to Crow Country: The Crow Place Name Project," pp. 111-116.

an affirmation and expression of Indigenous identity and validation of community held knowledge" (McCarty, 2000, p. 6). Literacy in the Native language is powerful in that it affects cultural learning across eras, from knowledge of history, literature and science in tribal times past, with children in today's classrooms (Bielenberg, 1999, p. 6).

Native language immersion schools are involved with the whole culture, and have delved into language learning through the music and artistry of the tribe (Boyer, 2000, p. 14). "Oral literature as curriculum . . . belongs to a real world setting that is natural, traditional, and imbued with its own set of meanings and ways of seeing" (Rubin, 1999, pp. 4-5). McCarty recounts the storytelling, drama, and arts that are learned through student participation with elder instructors in the Diné dwelling, during summertime literature camps (McCarty, 2000, p. 5). The place names site at Little Big Horn College associates stories, histories, and songs with the historical and cultural places through an interactive online database. Lodge Grass School on the Crow reservation in Montana sponsored a battle reenactment, a battle pivotal to the destiny of the Crow people. Crow children in the reenactment designed and constructed era-based regalia and an encampment. They retold the circumstance leading up to the battle, and recounted war deeds. Together with elders, they scripted the narrative, and interpreted the value and meaning of the battle. Warriors' leadership profiles were written in classes, and the songs of war, lullabies, and travel were sung (Real Bird, 2001, p. 21).

Broad-based community and tribal involvement is paramount to the planning and implementation of Native American language immersion schools. The public schools require considerable formal and official community involvement and policy development on behalf of the school boards and tribal governmental authorities. The private schools have developed through non-profit corporate status, and have entailed extensive legal, cultural, and financial structures. They have relied on long-term and solid community involvement and support. Parents participate in formal partnerships with the Native American language immersion schools. Often, parents are required to enroll in summer language immersion camps, to attend weekend language seminars, and participate in school activities as an extended family unit. Lac Courte Oreilles Ojibwe Immersion School has parent homework via audio and videotapes, to accompany student homework (M.F. Hermes, interview, October 19, 2001). The Piegan Institute requires tuition payments from parents, and parental loyalty to the principles of Blackfeet language learning—no English anywhere in the school, respect for elders, and more (Kipp, 2000, p. 15).

Quite literally, the Native American language immersion schools rely on the teamwork, cooperation, and commitment of elders, students, educators, parents, and community members (Rubin, 1999, p. 1). The commitment to language learning is one of major proportion. Darrell Kipp likens the commitment to the literal love that tribal elders have for their own grandchildren and great-grandchildren (Kipp, 2000, p. 7). This commitment is far beyond lip service to the principle of language learning. It means that tribal members must confront any issues attached to the language, and step up to actually "doing" language teaching and learning. Northern Cheyenne language scholar Richard Littlebear, president of Chief Dull Knife College, states, "The struggle in teaching and learning the tribal language is not with the children, it is with the adults. The adults have personal, often painful issues with their histories and experiences with formal education and the Native language."(R. Littlebear, interview, August 3, 2001).

Among the most difficult issues for tribal adults are those that connect Native language knowledge with negative school experiences. American Indian educational history is replete with negative associations. These associations have injured generations of American Indian people and promoted language loss. Community commitment and cooperation must move beyond the impact of these issues, and get to the firsthand work of language teaching *and* education; a new complex—one of promise. In a recent keynote speech, Darrell Kipp of the Piegan Institute observed that some tribal members are actually obstructionists. To them, he says: "If you can't help, then please, just get out of the way."

The Native American language immersion schools are funded in unique and dramatically different ways. For all of them, the challenge of respectable funding has been, is, and will be a challenge. How are they funded? The federal sources of support are categorical: the Bilingual Education for School Aged Children (part of the Elementary and Secondary Education Act) and the Native Languages Program of the Administration for Native Americans (U.S. Department of Health and Human Services). The U.S. Department of Education has bilingual education funding for language minority schools. Since the mid-1970s, this program has provided approximately 35 grants annually to schools serving American Indian children.

From inception, the bilingual education projects addressed Native language capacities in children, toward a language minority student population. Program formats and regulations have a bias toward Hispanic serving schools. In recent years, the program supports primarily "transition" project activities. Schools start language minority children in their primary language (Spanish or a Native language) and gradually build proficiency in English, the second language. The full transition to English as a medium of instruction is required to take place by the fifth grade.

Bilingual education as a transition program to English creates several dilemmas for tribal language immersion educators and activists. First, most tribal languages are the second languages for the Native school children. Second, the transition model is counter to objectives of tribal language acquisition through language immersion. Third, language immersion uses the Native language as the medium of education, hardly a fit for bilingual education (LaFortune, 2000, p. 18).

The Department of Health and Human Services, Administration for Native Americans (ANA), provides discretionary support for Native language revitalization projects. ANA projects follow a sequence: an assessment of fluency, selection of language intervention and revitalization methods (a relatively narrow number of methods acceptable), a planning year, and two years implementation of revitalization activities (C. Baker-Big Back, interview, August 8, 2001). Several ANA projects are Native American language immersion schools and camps. The ANA two-year operational grants are important start-up funds. Sustaining projects beyond that term is a challenge to grantees. The ANA is "in the unenviable position and some would say indefensible position of declining the majority of the increasing number of incoming grant proposals" (LaFortune, 2000, p. 17). The agency has important anecdotal information to share about project successes. And, while ANA grants have supported implementation, it cannot be counted on for the long-term, sustained support needed by Native American language immersion camps and schools.

Several Native language immersion schools are public schools. School boards, administrators, teachers, and parents have made a major decision to depart from mainstream instructional methods and strategies, and make a commitment to establish instruction in the tribal language. For these few districts, operational resources are available, but typically, the tax base that contributes funds to the school operations (beyond state foundation support) is slim to none, since a majority of Indian lands are non-taxable. Little or no start-up costs can be found. Continued support rests on student achievement based on mainstream standards established by the respective state and the locally elected school board.

The new charter school structure is the format of school organization for the Lac Courte Oreilles Ojibwe Language Immersion School. A federal initiative, the charter grant process is competitive. The charter provides a year of support for planning. Start-up support for parent and community interaction, supplies, and learning resources is available. But, start-up costs exclude the costs of building remodeling or acquisition. Operational funds are granted for a term of three to five years. The local school board must accept the concept and may place requirements on the charter school. At the LCO Language Immersion School, some of these conditions are: the right to non-renewal at strategic points during the five-year period and no tax-based district operational funds sharing. Public funds for schools are obligated to the routine school operations and few school districts are willing, or, for that matter, able to share their operational resources (Hermes, 2001, p. 2).

The school charter is an altogether new educational technology, and federal charters have become available only in the past few years. Nationally there are 800 charter schools with over 100,000 students, total. While in their inception and creation, they are highly creative and free from many of the mainstream school restrictions, the charter schools have a window of three to five years to achieve success, or experience charter revocation (Hadderman, 1998, p. 1). The Lac Courte Orielles Ojibwe Charter School director learned of the charter process through assisting a colleague who organized a charter magnet school for American Indian cultural learning in Minnesota.

Seventy percent of the charter schools are located in six states: Arizona, California, Colorado, Massachusetts, Michigan, Minnesota, and North Carolina. Clearly, this new avenue for school funding has potential importance for Native communities and school support. Private sector funding has been essential in the Piegan Institute of Montana. Several foundations have proven long-term partners through their support for the Blackfeet language immersion concept. Darrell Kipp, Piegan Institute development director, cites the generous support of the Lannan Foundation, the W.K. Kellogg Foundation, and the Grotto Foundation. But foundation support is difficult to acquire, and several factors present serious challenges for language immersion schools and projects. The factors surrounding private sector support for Native American language immersion and comprehensive language revitalization are discussed by Richard LaFortune in the Grotto Foundation publication, *Native Languages as World Languages: A Vision for Assessing and Sharing Information about Native Languages across Grant-Making Sectors*. These are important to enumerate, as private sector support is critical to the lifeline for Native American language immersion schools:

- Definitive information about Native American language immersion and its meaning to American Indian communities is lacking or located outside the reach of foundation decision-makers.

- Native communities have limited access to information about the private sector, and have few able grant writers to meet the standard of foundation leadership. Native language activists have school commitments that demand time and expertise, leaving little for fundraising. This is particularly true for activists who may be elders and traditional, and without professional certification and training in fund-raising techniques.

- Private sector grant making is often short term, and categorical. Short-term funding places the schools in a constant "funding hunt," and makes the quest for more funds an expense that takes precious resources from the actual teaching and learning activities. The categorical nature of private sector funds requires the schools to "fit" the foundation program. Sometimes the fit is difficult to achieve. Is Native language immersion a part of education, culture, community, or youth programming?

- Native communities have a fiscal balancing act between urgent social, educational, and economic issues that press limited tribal resources. The pressure on limited resources often leaves language immersion schools far down the tribal priority lists. Further, required matching funds are hard to identify and earn or obtain, when tribes' resources are severely limited.

- Fifty of the nation's 500 federally recognized tribes have profitable casino enterprises. These 50 have funding agendas of their own, and rarely extend to the remaining 450 tribes. Misperceptions about "casino tribes" cause troubling issues for fundraising and American Indians generally. One of the Native language immersion schools is funded by casino profits for a term period, the Southern Ute Preschool.

- Statistically, American Indians are less than 1% of the population of the United States. These proportionately small numbers often make American Indians invisible to nationally released educational studies. Studies do exist on educational, social, and economic indices, they are not as readily available or accessible, as are studies on predominant ethnic and racial group information.

All of these factors are complex. For the foundations, questions about American Indians, casinos, language immersion, education, culture and tribal priorities must and do arise. For the language immersion educators, questions about proposals, writing, narrowing the field to receptive organizations, and fitting into program priorities all exist. This study is a bridge for potential partners of Native American language immersion schools and projects.

LaFortune suggests that foundations can take a critical leadership role to "fortify the infrastructure of Native language networks" and help create alliances between the tribal communities and interested philanthropies. He encouraged foundations to become appraised of language preservation facts, and be responsive to the Native American language preservation initiatives. But, Native communities must also play a part in the leadership to strengthen the infrastructure of Native language networks by communicating "the validity of Indigenous methods of and attitudes toward organizing and transmitting traditional knowledge." Tribal groups must place education and language preservation among the highest tribal priorities (LaFortune, 2000, p. 33).

Immersion Camps

Immersion camps are most of the Native American language immersion activities happening now in the United States. The camps represent a broad range of language learning projects that focus on tribal language learning, on a short-term and time-concentrated basis. The tribal organizers select learning experiences in collaboration with tribal elders and members fluent in the language (Rubin, 1999, p. 2). Traditional Native activities are incorporated into the camp learning assignments (McCarty & Dick, 1996, p. 5). While most of the language immersion camps are convened in the summertime, many camps follow a cycle of activities within the seasons for rich language learning content and context (Rubin, 1999, p. 5). The immersion camps are especially successful in helping the students acquire "the smallest sounds of the language," as a foundation for "learning the big words" (R. Littlebear, interview, August 3, 2001).

Encampments feature tribal knowledge. The elders and tribal language instructors utilize the tribal oral literature, history, arts, music, and knowledge for learning experiences. Among the Native language immersion camp experiences are the new relationships established between and among the students and their instructors/activists. This relationship replicates the intimate kindred relations within the Native American extended family (Real Bird, 2000, p. 21). Camp participants are all ages. The camps are offered for varied time frames, from three days to four weeks. Camps are traditional encampments, set in tribal lands, a site chosen for rich language learning potential (Boyer, 2000, p. 14).

Immersion camps serve American Indian student groups ranging in size from 30 to 50 participants. Student learning teams are formed: 5 to 12 students team up with one or two educators/language instructors. The team is structured to interact, explore, discuss, discover, and experience. Some camps are designed for entire extended family units, for the learning teams (Real Bird, 2000, p. 2-3). The tribal colleges and universities have held numerous camps for their college students, their families, youth, and teacher trainees.

The Salish Kootenai College Cultural Leadership Project, the Chief Dull Knife College Cultural Apprenticeship Program, and the Three Affiliated Tribes of North Dakota Tribal Language Mentor Project are designed for cultural leadership development and incorporate the master/apprentice concept (Boyer, 2000, p. 14). The conduct of these projects often includes language immersion camps for children and youth as one component of a greater agenda for cultural leadership development. Section B-3 of this study is a discussion of the master/apprentice cultural leadership projects.

The immersion camp or retreat is a highly successful language learning approach for the Maori people of New Zealand, for youth and adults. The concept of short intense bursts of language learning in an immersion approach has promoted and developed a whole new generation of Maori speakers (Pease-Pretty On Top, 2002, p. 11). The weekend or whole week language learning seminars entail practical language learning, and teaches total fluency based on 10 words or phrases a session. Maori adults achieve remarkable daily language fluency in just four week-long seminars (24 hours a day for 7 days). The Maori call this "accelerated learning," and describe the learning as total brain involvement—movement, dancing, singing, and hands-on learning; no paper, no writing. The immersion camp model plays a special role with youth and young parents with the objective of conversational fluency (Pease-Pretty On Top, 2002, p. 13).

Native American communities, endeavoring in language immersion as a broader concept, will often begin their activities with camps, weeklong or weekend language intensive retreats or seminars. This learning approach is replicable due to the relatively short timeframe, the adaptability of content and context to seasonal traditional activities, and the high rate of language acquisition. Immersion camps are also chosen by Native American language immersion planning groups as awareness and commitment building activities that are significant in their own right, but are an important stepping stone to a greater commitment to a broader base of learning activities, such as month-long camps or language immersion schools. Further, the camp concept is accessible for reasons of cost. While cost is relative to the elaboration within the camp and number of participants, several sites have begun camps with tribal members and elders who volunteer their time, and interagency camp collaboration and sponsorship. For language acquisition, language immersion camps are viable and significant activities for Native American communities.

Immersion summertime experiences occur among teacher trainees, tribal colleges and universities students and faculty, university faculty, and general Native communities. At Bay Mills in Michigan, Ojibway people have convened a language teaching summer institute, for training Native language teachers for Ojibway public schools (Dale, 2000, pp. 8-10). University of Minnesota, Duluth faculty and students have a two-week language immersion learning opportunity with the university's Ojibway language faculty member (M.F. Hermes, interview, October 19, 2001). Fond du Lac Tribal and Community College teacher trainees (in Cloquet, Minnesota) attend a two-week summer language institute as part of their requirements for a bachelor's degree in teacher education (Stornberger, 2001, p. 1).

Students and community members at Little Priest Tribal College in Nebraska hold a three-week summertime Omaha language immersion camp for entire family groups.[4] The camp is combined with six weekends of immersion experiences—adults on Saturdays and the whole family with children on Sundays ("Little Priest," 2000, p. 28). There are perhaps as many as 20 immersion summer camps and experiences existing in Indian Country today whose efforts have been sustained for two or more years. The summer camps and experiences often serve multiple purposes: first, for language learning; second, for cultural learning; and third, for the broad-based community understanding of language immersion and its viability for the long-term. Summer sessions require a limited time frame and a fairly finite resource base.

Mentoring and Apprenticeships

Three sites are particularly designed for the development of language and cultural leaders. The concept of cultural leadership comes from the Native tradition of the cultural specialist. Many tribes have authorized cultural commissions and tribal colleges and universities have appointed eminent scholars in tribal studies. These designated commissioners and scholars agree to become

---

[4] See "Little Priest Tribal College Immerses Students in Language," pp. 109-110.

masters or mentors and arrange apprenticeships. Together, the mentor or master and apprentices organize their language and cultural learning over a period of years. Alongside the master, the apprentices acquire the tribal language, arts, songs, ceremonies, history, and more. The apprentices will become masters following the training period. In turn, a cascading effect may take apprentices on their own in their areas of language and culture. Three tribal colleges have chosen this approach to language learning: Chief Dull Knife College of the Northern Cheyenne in Montana, the Salish Kootenai College of the Salish Kootenai Confederated Tribes of Montana, and the Three Affiliated Tribes (Mandan, Arikara, and Hidatsa) of North Dakota.

The Salish Kootenai Confederated Tribes have selected an approach to language learning that combines a master of Salish language and culture, a cultural commissioner, with five apprentices. The apprentices are all outstanding students in the tribal college's Salish Kootenai studies program and are pursuing language teaching expertise. The master and apprentices convene during the seasons of the year and concentrate on summer learning opportunities. Over the past four years, the apprentices acquired expertise that is situated within the families and tribal communities, to "cascade" their knowledge, expertise, and leadership in the language and culture into and among the people, in the present and future.

The Three Affiliated Tribes of North Dakota have initiated a mentor/mentee project that addresses the three languages of their reservation, the Hidatsa, Mandan, and Arikara languages. Each language has a master and five apprentices; all apprentices are enrolled half time year-round at the Fort Berthold Community College in language and culture classes. All the apprentices are achieving formal language certification through the tribal council's legislated certification process. This is a complex project, with many levels of language and cultural learning with a cascading impact into the greater public, the schools, and the tribal communities (C. Baker-Big Back, interview, August 8, 2001).

Cultural relationships are significant and follow culturally viable and appropriate master/apprentice relationships from traditional Native ways of knowing and learning. Both projects illustrate the creative and unique Native approaches to language and culture revitalization, and their community-based principles for sustainability of tribal knowledge and expertise. Where there was one teacher or master, fully knowledgeable in the language and culture, now, with the master/apprenticeship projects, there are five specialists—eventually new masters. The potential is that each apprentice becomes a master and will arrange apprenticeships among the members of a new generation of Native people.

Tribal Elder's Role and Perspectives on Native Language Immersion

Tribal elders are essential to the life of Native language immersion schools, camps, and activities. In fact, the capacity of educators and activists to offer learning environments that are rich in language and culture literally rests on the involvement, cooperation and leadership of tribal elders.

Darrell Kipp of the Piegan Institute says it this way: "We use the analogy that the language is our grandparents" (Kipp, 2000, p. 67). Tribal elders play a heavy role in the development, planning, and implementation of language immersion schools, camps, and activities.

Navajo elders at Rough Rock Community School have tangible demonstrations of the way their lives can become the basis for school-based language and literacy learning. McCarty explains that the parents and grandparents want their children to learn the Navajo way of life, and therefore have developed a consciousness about the value of the Navajo language and culture (McCarty, 2000, p. 5). From traditional times to the present, Native elders have always held the most critical role in Native education, as teachers, role models, and mentors. Many of today's elders were directly taught by their grandparents, and had an optimal opportunity to learn firsthand the Native ways of knowing and learning, as well as acquire the language and culture of their people. In this way, today's elders have direct ties, knowledge, and experience that spans multiple generations: elders, their parents, their grandparents, and beyond. The elders of the 1930s and 1940s raised today's elders; they were children during the last decade of the buffalo days! Native communities have an extraordinary learning opportunity to involve elders in teaching and learning. Rich teaching methods of the traditional Native extended family engender children and learners of all ages in the language and culturally based knowledge. This traditional Native method connects the generations (Pease-Pretty On Top, 2000, p. 1).

Native language immersion classrooms, camps, and activities have structured intergenerational learning that promotes language learning, cultural participation, and builds new and life-long human relationships. Teresa McCarty recounts the value of this relationship: "Schools and their participants that can support and safeguard the integrity of that (Native) socio-cultural environment...by fostering the sharing of language experiences between young and old is indeed a powerful tool."(McCarty, 2000, p. 6).

Educators created the Brockton Public School kindergarten and first grade, a Nakoda language immersion school, and utilize the Montessori method of instruction because, "it is an approach that has been around for centuries in Native culture" (Real Bird, 2001, p. 21). Tribal elders provide the learning content and context for Native language learning environments, as a "living experience"; they directly provide a wealth of information as well as "understanding values" (Mistaken Chief, 1999, p. 26). Elder involvement in Native language immersion camps, classrooms, and activities is multi-dimensional and integral to the language learning in tribal communities.

The vitality of the Native language immersion effort rests heavily on the vitality of the language speakers, and most of the speakers are tribal elders. Several issues arise from this reliance on elders; these issues pose complex challenges for Native language immersion projects. First, tribal elders may have extensive language and cultural knowledge, but have mixed or limited interests to share knowledge outside the confines of their own extended family or immediate community. Second, the personal circumstance of the elder may not lead to teaching, especially if the elder has already become retired. Third, many elders have health issues that limit their activity or stamina in general; camps and classrooms are often physically demanding. Finally, elders may harbor attitudes that limit positive involvement in learning and teaching, like teasing or making fun of new language learners, or modeling resentment, sadness, or anger, related to the loss of tribal language (Littlebear, 1999, p. 20). These issues occur in the language immersion planning and advisory committees, and must be addressed as they arise.

What happens when there are no elders for language immersion teaching? For some of the Native language immersion schools it has been necessary to search nationally or internationally for elders or teachers. Many of the Native tribes reside on multiple reservations and have membership living in nearby cities. For example, the Lac Courte Oreilles Ojibwe Preschool conducted a successful search for Ojibway language immersion teachers by searching into Manitoba reserves (Williams, 2001, p.1). On the Northern Plains, Lakota people reside in six states on over 10 reservations and many urban locations. While educators note the possible dialectical differences, they say there may be no choice. The project may successfully search outside the immediate community for the essential component, the tribal elders or language speakers, although it's not an easy task. For smaller tribes, alternatives may be narrow. In North Dakota, the Arikara tribal educators have opted for technology applications of language learning. Where the language loss rate needs "life support" technology may be the only answer for Native language immersion experiences.

As a means of building community vitality, Native language immersion is an enormous source of intergenerational relationships. New and focal attention is given to the tribal elders, their knowledge in language and culture and abilities in Native ways of knowing and learning. The children of the Piegan Institute have forged a new and durable relationship with the Blackfeet elders, typified by activist Darrell Kipp: "Many things transferred in our religion and our tribal ways come to us because of our knowledge of the language. . . . There is much to be said about immersion—more than what goes on in the schoolroom" (Kipp, 2000, p. 14).

Native American Language Immersion Teachers

Who are the Native language immersion teachers? The teachers in practice right now are primary speakers of their tribal language. The speaking ability is their sole common characteristic. By profession and vocation, they represent varied levels of education and training. In immersion schools, teachers are retired administrators, teacher aids, facilities managers, ranchers and grandparents. Kipp of the Piegan Institute notes that some of their best teachers were classified employees of the public schools (Kipp, 2000, p. 14).

Littlebear of the Northern Cheyenne Language Immersion Camp advises about finding teachers: "You have to start with what you've got. It never gets any better than today; tomorrow is worse" (R. Littlebear, interview, August 3, 2001). The Native language immersion committees and advisory boards carefully identify from among the community qualified fluent speakers and begin from there. The teachers (educators or activists) are all ages, although elders predominate among them.

The language immersion teaching demands a high level of physical stamina, knowledge of the tribal language and culture, and the capacity to help advance students to meet educational objectives (Howard & Loeb, 1998, p. 1). The Native language immersion schools now operating rely heavily on the tribal culture for the content and context of learning in the classroom. The Native language immersion teacher must have a comprehensive understanding of the tribal culture, as well as being informed about community members who can serve as language and culture resources for supplementing their own expertise. The Native language immersion teacher facilitates guest speaker presentations and field experiences to visit tribal elders and role models. The total physical response method utilizes movement, motion, and gesture in the early stages of language learning, and demands general physical fitness of the teachers. Native language immersion teachers must have a grasp of learner-centered approaches, interactive strategies, cultural immersion activities, home study materials, and supplemental parent learning activities (Rubin, 1999, pp. 7–11).

Field, discovery, and experiential learning activities are integral to language immersion learning. Teachers must be informed and knowledgeable of sacred, historic, and natural tribal sites. Connecting students to these significant sites demands complex skills of the teacher. The teacher must have the where-with-all to transport the children safely, make provision for appropriate food, materials, and sanitation, and create learning activities that build the full appreciation of the site for subject information, as well as language acquisition (R. Littlebear, interview, August 3, 2001). School and camp directors have addressed this complex challenge by using a teaching team strategy. Some schools have a logistics coordinator assigned to the multitude of important details for this type of learning activity effectiveness (C. Baker-Big Back, interview, August 8, 2001). The approach to experiential learning is also addressed by keeping the student to teacher ratio relatively low: fewer than 10 students to one teacher. Holistic learning activities, rich in field and experiential aspects, are complex and challenging to the teacher's coordination and teamwork talents.

Additional qualities that language immersion teachers must have include strong interpersonal skills and sensitivity to new language learners (who make frequent mistakes). Parents and grandparents are incorporated into the learning activities; this requires both coordination and sensitivity. Schools require parental involvement and learning, and the teachers must make their involvement meaningful and facilitate language experiences that advance the parents and support the language learning of their students.

Native language immersion projects have jointly sponsored training in total physical response through experts like Dr.

Richard Littlebear and Darrell Kipp. The Piegan Institute convened practitioners of language immersion twice, in 2000 and 2001 for technical assistance and training. Most projects have sent coordinators and teachers to other existing sites for weeklong observations and direct interaction with practicing teachers. The conduct of Native language immersion schools and camps requires intricate planning and careful implementation on site among teachers and project/school advisors. In addition, many schools have held summer seminars to create lesson plans (Dale, 2000, pp. 22-23).

Most tribal colleges and universities have tribal language courses within their tribal studies curriculum, and half have tribal studies degrees with language as an emphasis. Many of the tribes with TCUs have established the tribal language as the official language of the nation (Rubin, 1999, p. 5). In North Dakota, Montana, and Arizona, state legislatures established a process for the certification of tribal language teachers. The certification of tribal language teachers (within the system) typically includes tribal language courses, letters of reference from tribal language speakers, recognition by the tribal culture commission, and a satisfactory test of competence in the language. The combination of tribal colleges' courses and degrees, tribal official language status, and state/school recognition of a certification process for language teachers has contributed to the development of language immersion teachers in several locations.

The Three Affiliated Tribes of North Dakota are an example of this combination of factors. Fort Berthold Community College[5] students enroll in language courses and major in tribal studies. They complete requirements for language teacher certification as established by the tribes. As apprentices to tribal language masters they assist in ceremonies and events, and serve as tribal language teachers in the schools (C. Baker-Big Back, interview, August 8, 2001). The tribal language initiatives are multi-faceted in most of the Native language immersion project locations, and

---

[5] Fort Berthold Community College changed its name to Nueta Hidatsa Sahnish College in 2015.

indicate the level of grassroots effort from tribal language activists and educators to "grow your own" teachers (McCarty, 2000, p. 4).

Spiritual Connotations and Transformative Impacts of Native Language Immersion

Native language immersion schools, camps and activities have dimensions that are both spiritual and transformative. Native language immersion activist Kipp notes the spiritual dimension of language and culture learning for the children at Piegan Institute and the eldest women's society. "Many things transferred in our religion and our tribal ways come to us because of our knowledge of the language."(Kipp, 2000, p. 4).

Crow Indian scholar Lanny Real Bird describes how the language teachers and elders provide cultural practices and experiences that convey "values, protocol, and holistic awareness that include spiritual and traditional philosophical teachings" (Real Bird, 2001, p. 12). Language learning, in the whole cultural context, is "communicative, natural, interactive, creative, subtle, powerful, and metaphoric" (Rubin, 1999, p. 2). Indigenous educator Kalena Silva sees the critical connection between land, lineage, language, and culture for Native peoples, and states about this connection: "A bond born out of respect, the bond links to ancestors as well as to future generations" (Silva, 2000, pp. 71-73). Silva further analogizes, "language and culture provide physical, spiritual, and emotional sustenance, the strength of which depends on the riches of the soil where it grows." Native scholars note the nature and influence of language immersion learning within the tribal cultural context, and confirm learning opportunities that are spiritual and transformative.

Native language immersion teachers (educators and activists) are often cultural leaders in the Native community. The value of their role in language teaching is in essence, "medicine...of traditional education, for the wellbeing and health of the community" (Real Bird, 2001, p. 15). Tribal language fluency is held in such high regard, and the teachers are regarded as "keepers of medicine." This concept is shared among tribes, as

Blackfeet educator and activist Betty Bastien says, "The viewpoint in the language has the power to heal ourselves" (Mistaken Chief, 1999, p. 27).

The Big Picture in Native Education and Native Language Preservation

Native language immersion is part of a broader and more comprehensive effort to preserve Native American languages. Native language preservation efforts include dictionary and lexicon projects, modern language and bilingual education classes in school settings, curriculum development projects, technology-based presentations of tribal language, images, and linguistic studies of the Native languages. Language immersion contrasts with these in that the use of the Native language is the medium of communication and instruction about the tribal and mainstream knowledge. The essential purpose of immersion is to build fluency in the tribal language among the participants. Tribal groups across the nation are involved in many language preservation efforts. These are reviewed in the LaFortune study, a publication of the Grotto Foundation of St. Paul, Minnesota.

The policy of the tribal nations is most significant in the preservation of tribal languages. "Tribal initiative and control are essential to the success of renewal efforts...it is crucial for Native speakers to see the value of doing so (saving the language) and get actively involved in the process" (Crawford, 1994, p. 5). The official affirmation of the language and culture are "key decisions regarding the preservation and teaching" of the tribal language (Rubin, 1999, p. 1). The official acts, the policies, establish the authority to train and certify language teachers, build unity and commitment to language revitalization, and provide guidance for planning, development, implementation, and evaluation of new language programs (Rubin, 1999, p. 1). The Administration for Native Americans' language reservation projects are contingent on tribal policy (Demmert & Arnold, 1996, p. 2). Tribal policy is significant to the language immersion projects for support, commitment, and official guidelines and intent.

The U.S. Secretary of Education, Cavazos, appointed the Indian Nations at Risk Task Force in 1989. The Indian Nations at Risk (INAR) report, published in 1991, mandated that "Native children must have equal schooling early in the educational process for learning their Native languages as well as for learning English and other languages." About teachers, the report stated, "Indian students must have early access to teachers that are proficient Native American language speakers, who are capable of expanding the dimensions of tribal languages into content areas such as math, science, social studies, arts, and vocational applications" (Demmert & Arnold, 1996, p. 2).

Tribal language learning was Goal 2 of the INAR report for the improvement of Native educational performance. The Native Languages Act of 1990, P.L. 101-447, declares "Native Americans have the right to use their languages and it is a U.S. government policy to preserve, protect, promote the development of Native American languages" (Demmert & Arnold, 1996, p. 2). Amendments to the Native Languages Law in 1992 established grant programs to tribes and organizations to support a wide range of activities aimed at ensuring Native language survival. Competitive grants were made available through the executive department, Health and Human Services Administration for Native Americans. Additional grant funds were made available through the National Park Service, Keepers of the Treasures Program, and the National Endowment for the Humanities (Demmert & Arnold, 1996, p. 2). The Department of Education administers the Bilingual Education Act, Title VII of Improving America's Schools Act of 1994. Bilingual Education funds have contributed support to the general tribal language preservation projects in public schools nationwide.

Several states have made certification provisions for Native language teaching and for the acceptance of tribal language learning as a modern language credit. North Dakota, Montana, and Arizona Public Instruction Officers have arranged through joint organization, processes for tribal language competency and literacy levels, and respective level testing procedures (Boyer, 2000, p. 12). Tribes have established course and experience requirements and taken the major responsibility to train and assess language teachers. The policy for language teacher certification comes from decades of tribal language promotion by tribal leaders and educators with state legislators and state offices of public instruction.

Native American language immersion is rare within the public school structure. The Diné (Navajo) two-way language immersion schools at Round Rock, Rough Rock, and Chinle schools in Arizona are supported via the state schools' foundation funds, and locally generated categorical funding (Howard & Sugarman, 2001, p. 1). The charter school organized for Lac Courte Oreilles Ojibwe language immersion is a part of the Hayward School District of Hayward, Wisconsin. Most of the language immersion schools are privately supported. Because public school structure is highly regulated and relatively inflexible, the majority of language immersion school organizers have chosen a private school structure.

The public schools in the United States are English language based with prescribed curricula and certified teachers. In contrast, Native American language immersion schools are Native language based with Native American and mainstream curricula and tribally qualified/certified teachers, primarily tribal scholars. The three Diné communities and the Ojibway people of Hayward achieved a unity of purpose about language immersion among the school board members, educational leaders, teachers and staff, parents, and students. A completely new approach and methodology replaced the traditional mainstream one. At Hayward, the school board agreed to allocate classroom space to the language immersion school, but withheld the state foundation support (Hermes, 2001, p. 2). The charter school support is primarily federal. The public schools are in fact English language based, although, in theory, the American public school could be "Native language based." These Native American communities have established valuable precedents for public school potential.

The Native Hawaiian language immersion schools demonstrate the full realm of possibility. The Ke Kula Kaiapuni schools are organized within the public school structures among numerous public school districts. Language immersion organizers acquired their schools or streams within the larger schools one step at a time, one grade at a time. Over a 25 year period, the Native Hawaiian people orchestrated the development of Native Hawaiian curriculum, certified teachers and school structures. Still, in each new language nest and language immersion school, parents and community members have demonstrated profound commitment, organization, and sacrifice for language immersion on behalf of their children. Combined, state regulations, local school control, published and prescribed curricula, and standard teacher certification form a formidable recalcitrance to change. Native Hawaiian people have made remarkable language immersion inroads into the public school system (on a trail of blood, sweat, and tears), and established a remarkably effective model for Native Americans and Indigenous people.

The tribal colleges' mission has at its heart the preservation of tribal languages, cultures and histories. Over half of the nation's tribally controlled colleges and universities sponsor language immersion preschools, camps, schools, and/or teacher training programs. Several of these are featured in this study. Tribal colleges are chartered by their respective nations. Thirty-two colleges are located in 12 states. Tribal colleges and universities serve more than 26,000 full- and part-time American Indian students from over 250 tribes. All of these institutions are fully accredited or working toward accreditation through the regional accreditation process. Degrees and certificates are offered in fields of study that are reflective of the tribal nations' economy and society. All 32 colleges offer associate's degrees (two-year); half offer bachelor's degrees and four offer graduate-level studies and degrees. Tribal college students are typically older and family responsible. Both public and private resources support the tribal colleges. The tribal colleges are especially community based and have programs in community, youth and parent development. The fields of education, human services, health, business, and the sciences are several curriculum areas offered by the tribal colleges. Many sponsor preschools or daycare centers and are deeply involved in programming for school-aged American Indian children (Gipp, 2003, p. xiii).

The tribal colleges consortium for federal relations and development is the American Indian Higher Education Consortium (AIHEC). Since 1972, the consortium has provided essential and united leadership for tribal college development. AIHEC has partnered with congressional leaders to develop the Tribally Controlled Community College Assistance Act of 1978 (operational support for the colleges), the Land Grant Status Act of 1994 (USDA-related programs development) and the White House Initiative on Tribal Colleges and Universities—an executive order of the United States president (partnerships with executive branch agencies). The tribal colleges' consortium for private sector relations and development is the American Indian College Fund. Since 1989, the fund's purpose is to raise private sector awareness and resources for tribal college student scholarships, cultural and language programs, and an endowment. Extensive tribal college information is provided at AIHEC and the Fund's websites. Links to the tribal colleges are also available.

The U.S. Department of Health and Human Services administers the Head Start Programs. An initiative for preschool education from the 1960s War on Poverty, Head Start is an integral part of education for many American Indian tribes. The Administration for Native Americans manages the Indian Head Start programs language immersion initiatives, and bilingual approaches exist among the Indian Head Start programs, to a limited extent.

As a part of the Indian Self-Determination Act of 1975, tribal nations may contract Bureau of Indian Affairs schools serving their reservations. Contracts may also support previously parochial schools on the reservations. Approximately 40 tribes have contracted schools under this authority, and provide community based and local control principles of school management and direction. Tribal schools successfully recruit and retain American Indian teachers and incorporate language and culture as a major component of school curriculum. These schools have demonstrated academic successes with their students. Two

Eagle River School is a contracted tribal school of the Salish Kootenai Confederated Tribes of Montana. Saint Frances Indian School is another tribal school, formerly a Catholic school, of the Rosebud Sioux Nation of South Dakota. Saint Frances Indian School provides a Lakota language immersion stream for grades K-6. (A. Whitehat, interview February 11, 2003). The community and parental control aspects of tribal and contract schools may provide a place for Native American language immersion schools or streams within schools.

Native Language Immersion Projects

Native language immersion projects serve Native adults and children in 50 tribal locations. For the purposes of this research, interviews and observations (where feasible) have been conducted. The interviews and observations became a research priority from its initial stages due primarily to the unique and distinguishing qualities of each language immersion project. These qualities are a function of the project leadership, leadership from coordinators and advisory group members, from the students and the support of the greater Native community. Each project is in fact a composite whole, both by design and as it operates daily, in a most practical sense. Language immersion is inextricably tied to the tribal language speakers, most often elders.

The summer language immersion camp for the Northern Cheyenne of southeastern Montana was held in the Wolf Teeth Mountains. The students range in age from 7 to 20 years of age. Linguist and educator Richard Littlebear, president of Chief Dull Knife College, says, "Language learning is organic and holistic, and therefore, we work with a broad range of ages." The student teacher ratio is 5:1; a standard set after several years of experience trying other ratios and learning arrangements. In the fifth year of the immersion camp, the language immersion was coming together, with a set of methods and practices that fit the camp setting and the instructors. Dr. Littlebear explains that "they had the freedom to move into language immersion methods by trial and error...to be creative and innovative."

The students stay for two weeks, with their instructors. They live in tents and teepees, pitched in a scenic mountain site encircled with pines on a huge 20-acre grassy valley. Learning the Northern Cheyenne language rests on the learning team, the team of Cheyenne language educators. The team has a planning session for two-weeks prior to the camp. The educators study the total physical response method of language teaching. As scholars of the language and culture, the language immersion team members are recognized in the Northern Cheyenne tribe of Montana. Littlebear recounts that "staff and instructors must take the time for team building," and the planning sessions keep that as a focus as well. "The program design is a function of these two things: the degree of assimilation and the degree of language loss. The DKMC staff and instructors are relatively young, and their stamina can be relied upon for many years. The younger speakers' youth and health give the program intensity and allow activity oriented programming." Staff members are assigned the logistics of meals and snacks, transportation, tents and teepee construction, materials and equipment ordering, and management.

The project advisors meet year round, with the Chief Dull Knife College vice-president for culture, Conrad Fisher. The Northern Cheyenne Culture Commission is the project advisory group. The commission members are the elders who keep the language and tradition for the Northern Cheyenne Nation. Littlebear narrates: "The advisory group, especially elders and district representatives, provide their ideas on the camp and on language certification. The advisors group is a means of political buy-in as well as general community support." In the immersion camp, each language immersion educator and five or six children form a learning group. These learning groups maintain consistent membership throughout the camp period. The groups meet concurrently and implement learning activities chosen by the educators. The educators are various ages and both men and women. One group hikes around the camp periphery and learns the flora and fauna near the camp. A second group makes miniature rawhide shields and discusses family relationships. Yet another makes intricate beaded jewelry and listens to an educator's childhood experiences. From a central vantage point, the observer viewed five additional learning groups studying, interacting, and learning. Northern Cheyenne language is the medium of discussion. Students listen intently and repeat phrases during the discussions. Between four and seven hours are spent in the small group learning each day.

Camp learning takes place in activities for the whole group, as well as in the learning groups. Presentations by Cheyenne scholars instruct on tribal history and culture. For example, all the campers participated in the buffalo butchering. The camp received a gift of a buffalo. Camp directors chose to make this gift a learning experience. Together, educators and students learned buffalo anatomy; cut and dried buffalo meat; constructed drying scaffolds; and planned, prepared, and served a traditional feast to elders and guests.

The Crazy Head Springs encampment is a camping facility owned by the Mennonite Church, used for youth and family camps. The Chief Dull Knife College, primary sponsor of the language immersion camp, leases the camp. Here, a pine grove rims a huge meadow. The trees and adjoining acreage provide shade and are ideal for outdoor classroom locations, for hiking and exploration. The central gathering area for assemblies and food service are under an enormous awning stretched over a metal framework. This central gathering area is the stage for history and literature telling, by elder guests. Walking trails lead around and through the camp area; one trail leads to a nearby spring.

The camp setting, the prepared and intense language instruction, the learning group experiences, the relationships among the children with the educators, the camp assemblies and field experiences, all contribute to a rich language immersion environment. The camp demonstrates conversations and interactions with and among the students—in the Cheyenne language about Cheyenne knowledge (R. Littlebear, interview, August 3, 2001).

Fond du Lac Community and Tribal College in Cloquet, Minnesota, sponsors a teacher training project. The project is based on best practices from Indian education and enrolls 25 tribal members in teacher training. A year-round cohort of trainees combines standard professional teacher training for Minnesota teachers and college students with Ojibway culture, language, and history. The Ojibway language is required in the professional training. Each season "the trainees have a camp or retreat pertaining to the season-specific cultural knowledge of the Ojibway people.

Tribal member and project director Amy Bergstrom describes the annual summer language immersion camp: "The pre-service teachers take a one-week long language immersion camp and learn a remarkable amount of Ojibway...their minds are like sponges." The camp was held in a remote location in Ojibway country. Through music and art activities, the teacher trainees acquired a rich Ojibway cultural context for language learning. Although many of the students had enrolled in high school Ojibway language courses, their fluency was limited to "vocabulary lists, numbers, and names of things." The language immersion camp was located in the mountains. For a whole week, the trainees camped together, 24 hours per day for seven days, and all their communications were in Ojibway. From Ms. Bergstrom: "In the morning, we have an informal time with the instructor. In the afternoon, we have traditional activities—bread making, berry picking. In the evening, we hike and visit tribal resource people. We want to have language use at all times" (A. Bergstrom, interview, October 18, 2001).

During the academic year, the trainees enroll in a more standard Ojibway language class at the community college, with the same instructor (as the immersion camp). Wintertime learning activities include tribal history, a snowshoe field trip, and tribal elder presentations. Together, the trainees prepared Ojibway learning cards on common verbs and conversational vocabulary. The trainees authored and illustrated a children's book called the *Sugar Bush Kids*, with artwork, activities, and a story about Ojibway children. This wintertime learning will prepare them for next summer's camp.

Reflecting on the initial two project years, Ms. Bergstrom says, "Each camp and retreat we have, there is less and less English, and more Ojibway language. I attribute this language capacity of the trainees to an Ojibway-rich environment." She cites the improved confidence levels of the students, making presentations in Ojibway, and noted the intensity and enthusiasm of the trainees.

The Three Affiliated Tribes of North Dakota have initiated a mentor/mentee project that addresses the three languages of the Three Affiliated Tribes of North Dakota, the Hidatsa, Mandan, and Arikara languages. Each of the languages has a master with five apprentices. All the apprentices (15) are enrolled halftime and year round at the Fort Berthold Community College. They are majors in tribal language and culture that is part of the tribal studies program at the Associate of Arts level. All the apprentices aim to achieve formal language certification through the tribes' certification process for tribal language instruction. There are many levels of language and culture learning in this project.

All these have an impact on language learning. It can best be described as a "cascading" language immersion project, for concurrently with the mentoring from the masters of language and culture, the apprentices are language teachers in the schools serving the tribal children and youth. This project has several positive advantages for language learning: 1.) The apprentices become cultural and language specialists over time, and serve the communities in this capacity for the rest of their lives. Since most of them are 30 years old, many years of service can be anticipated. 2.) The apprentices are involved first hand on a daily basis with the Mandan, Arikara, and Hidatsa children enrolled in the schools. As their instructors and cultural advisors, they are well known by the new generation of tribal members. Their influence in language learning and cultural knowledge is well established. 3.) The schools have made a commitment to provide a significant position for language teaching and learning in the public school curriculum and among the faculty. 4.) The master has the opportunity to train several successors in cultural and language leadership. The masters have assistants in carrying out their demanding family, community and cultural role (C. Baker-Big Back, interview, August 8, 2001). This approach is similar to a cultural apprenticeship project at Chief Dull Knife College of the

Northern Cheyenne in Montana and the cultural leadership project of Salish Kootenai College of the Salish Kootenai Confederated Tribes of Montana.

The Iñupiaq Immersion School, Nikaitchuat Ilisagviat, is a private school for children ages three to seven years old. Four teachers manage the learning in the school, and the learning is exclusively in the Iñupiaq language and has a culture-based curriculum. The school hours are from 7:30 a.m. to 3:30 p.m. daily. The school is not associated with the public school, and funds for the school (in part) are acquired through tuition ($350/month).

Nikaitchuat was started by a "vital team [that] consisted of 30 parents, grandparents, and community members who were concerned about the state of our Iñupiaq language and culture." For years, the team met, but in the spring of 1998, the group leaders Tarruq and Agnik Schemer and 10 team members accepted tasks that led to the start of the school. "The school opened in the fall of 1998, with a building, teachers, parents, and a group of children ready to learn; and $100 for materials and supplies." In the spring of 2000, Nikaitchuat received a grant from the U.S. Department of Education for staff, office equipment, and materials development. This grant added to an initial budget comprised of funds from BIA-Johnson O'Malley, Alaskan Native Corporation support, parent tuition, and a health initiative grant.

Parental involvement begins with the payment of monthly tuition. Parents provide a daily snack once a month, and "volunteer for four hours per month...help in the classroom, attend parent meetings, participate in sewing nights, and attend Eskimo dance practice."

A seven member Parent Governance Committee helps in the direction of the school. "The school curriculum calendar was produced with the guidance of local elders and other community members. In three parts: 1.) the daycare "Big Book," filled with Western topics such as letters, colors, numbers, and shapes; 2.) traditional activities based on the Iñupiaq lifestyle, including hunting, fishing, berry-picking, gathering plants, dancing, drumming, and transportation; and 3.) Iñupiaq values. The calendar is seasonal, having a specific cultural content each month of the school year. For example, in March the topics are "transportation, cars and trucks, airplanes, snow machines, and dog sleds." Elders and community members are instructors and host field experiences for the students (Iñupiaq Immersion School, 2001, pp. 1-10). The school focuses on the Iñupiat Illitqusiat, the values. These are comprehensive and reflect the Iñupiaq way of life.

In 1998, Lac Courte Orielles Ojibwa Community College opened a preschool for tribal children, an Ojibway language immersion school. Six to 10 children attended the school designed to replicate "an Ojibwa grandma's house." Instructor William Wilson describes the instructional method, "We talk to and with the children, in intensive interaction. For example we take the children for a walk in the woods near the school, and talk with them in Ojibwa (no English), about everything we see." Wilson cites the quick learning he has experienced among the youngest students: "The younger students understand Ojibwa right away, you can see it." The children are three to five years old.

Lac Courte Orielles Ojibwa Community College sought fluent Ojibwa instructors and met with frustration locally. The search turned up few applicants. The Ojibwa people live far and wide in the Great Lakes region of the U.S. and Canada. The college eventually retained two Ojibwa people from Manitoba who agreed to move to Hayward, Wisconsin, for two years for the project. The premium of fully fluent instructors was accomplished, and promoted the language learning. Instructor Wilson narrated the assistance they received from elders in the community: "Elders in the community, they do help us with our classes, they come to the school and talk with the children" (W. Wilson, interview, May 11, 2001).

The Lac Courte Orielles Ojibwe Language Immersion Charter School is located in Hayward, Wisconsin. The school is in its second year of operation. The school director, Dr. Mary Fong Hermes, described the school's beginning: "We pursued the K-12 charter last spring, 2001. This charter school would continue the work of the LCO Language Immersion Preschool, a three-year program of the LCO Tribal and Community College. Our aim is to provide a K-12 Ojibwa language immersion school." Dr. Hermes was a full-time teacher in the Hayward Public Schools, and then became involved in the language immersion preschool initiative. Now, she serves as the part-time school director.

The LCO Ojibwa Language Immersion Charter School currently serves children in kindergarten through third grade. A coordinating and advisory committee carried out a planning year, and Dr. Hermes says, "We are beginning the first year of the school with these grades, with two full-time teachers who came over from the public school and one fulltime Ojibwa language teacher. The teachers know the standard school curriculum." Most of the 20 students in the school were enrolled in the immersion preschool during the past several years.

The LCO Language Immersion School is situated within the Hayward Public Schools. The school board has provided approval for the immersion school, and as a condition for the charter, lent fiscal support from the state allocations for foundation school funding to the fledgling school. Parents of the children made written commitments to their children's enrollment, and have subsequently enrolled their children in the school. The board discussion entailed concerns, for example, "board members expressed a concern that language teaching would be done at the expense of another required subject." For the LCO Language Immersion School, board support was acquired in a 5:1 favorable vote.

The charter is a federal designation, and provides a stream of federal support from the Department of Education. For a five-year period, start up and operational financial sustenance combined with the state foundation funds. Dr. Hermes cited limitations, "The funding acquired excludes a building and/or renovation of a second-hand building." This limitation made it necessary to borrow a classroom from the public school. Other services, like lunch and health services, will be shared with the public school. The charter gives organizers, instructors, and students a period of grace from state testing routines, while the curriculum with students has a chance for establishment and elaboration. Tests will be taken in the third year and continuation is contingent on successful educational outcomes.

The Crow Indian people, or the Apsaalooke, reside on a reservation nearly as large as Connecticut. An historic leader and visionary, Arapooish led the Apsaalooke on a 40-year migration from Minnesota through Oklahoma and then Canada through the Great Salt Lake region to the Big Horn Mountains of present day Wyoming and Montana. Here, the visionary saw the stars fall on a sacred plant, tobacco. The migration trail and the Crow land and water serve as the primary cultural and historic context and content for the Crow language immersion camp, the Crow Land and Water Migration Camp. The camp, built of teepees and tents, was located near the "star falling place" in the southern part of the Crow Indian reservation near the border between Wyoming and Montana. The camp moved twice, to other Crow country locations in the Pryor Mountains, the range just west of the Big Horn Mountains. Crow language expert, Dr. Lanny Real Bird, and a team of fluent Crow language speakers, Roy Stewart, Scott Russell, Jennifer Flat Lip and Mandy Moccasin, and Crow Indian science teacher Shane Doyle, designed the Crow language immersion camp experience for 30 Crow Indian youth. Guest presenters were brought into the camp each day. The purpose of the Land and Water Migration Camp was threefold, and includes building the land and water knowledge in Crow Indian students in the fourth to eighth grades. In a total language immersion environment for Crow language learning, these activities are developed into lesson plans for classroom teachers. The coordinating team partnered with the Montana State University Indian Teacher Training Project in Billings.

The teacher trainees participated as camp counselors and learning activity assistants. Students, counselors, and instructors were encouraged to utilize the Crow language at all times throughout the camp. Students fluent in the Crow language were paired up with non-Crow language speaking students to form learning partnerships. For the instructors, the science teacher teamed with a translator for presentations on the land and water. The curriculum provided learning activities: lectures on land and water topics (English, then Crow), demonstrations of teepee construction, presentations on tribal history and culture in the Crow language, guest and elder presenters, site visits to historic and traditional sites, and water testing in mountain springs and streams.

The summer of 2001 was the initial language immersion camp. The Crow Land and Water Migration Camp was experimental, and successfully involved several groups. These groups were the teacher trainees, the students, the advisors and elders, and the instructors and counselors (C. Old Elk, interview, April 17, 2001).

The Piegan Institute was organized by Darrell Kipp and a small group of fellow Blackfeet tribal members. Together, "They longed to go home again, to reconnect with their culture and relearn the language they'd spoken as children." The Piegan Institute is a nonprofit organization on the Blackfeet Indian Reservation, dedicated to restoring and preserving Native American languages (Nijhuis, 2002). In 1995, the institute opened the privately funded Nizipuhwahsin (or Real Speak) Center, which immerses students in the Blackfeet language from kindergarten through eighth grade. The school's graduates are the first young fluent speakers of the Blackfeet language in a generation. Nizipuhwahsin teacher Shirlee Crow Shoe says the school is not only resuscitating the language, but also helping to preserve Blackfeet culture.

The institute has three kindergarten through eighth grade language immersion schools: Cuts Wood, Moccasin Flat, and Lost Child. The first eighth grade class is scheduled to graduate is 2003. The schools have a student/teacher ratio of 7:1, which Kipp commends, "Individual attention from specially trained staff helps push them ahead of their peers in achievement tests" (Selden, 2000, p. 1).

Shirlee Crow Shoe, a Nizipuhwahsin teacher, says about her students: "They will put their hands out and introduce themselves to you in Blackfeet. Learning the language has clarified their identity." Today, the Nizipuhwahsin Center has 36 students and more applicants than it can accept.

The immersion models from the Maoris in New Zealand and Native Hawaiians instructed the center organizers. They were especially influenced by the "language nests," systems that have since been extended through the 12th grade. The immersion school model from the Akwesasne Freedom School in upstate New York, also demonstrated success. From these models, Kipp and the rest of the staff at the Piegan Institute thought immersion could bring back the Blackfeet language.

The Piegan Institute has played a leading role in providing three gatherings of language immersion scholars from Indian country. Director Darrell Kipp has stepped forward with a narrative for language immersion organizers and activists. The model of the Piegan Institute's immersion schools demonstrates to Native people, especially in the United States, that language immersion can be accomplished. Kipp and his colleagues are adamant that private sector funding is the exclusive resource for the schools' support, along with tuition paid by parents and family.

The Salish Kootenai Confederated Tribes of Montana have selected an approach to language immersion learning that combines a master of Salish language and cultures and tribally designated cultural commissioners, with five apprentices. The apprentices are tribal members, and younger than the masters. The apprentices are all outstanding students in the Salish Kootenai College tribal studies Associate of Arts degree program. The master and apprentices convene throughout the seasons of the year, and concentrate on summer learning opportunities. Over the past four years, the apprentices have acquired expertise that is situated within the families and tribal communities. This approach provides a way to "cascade" their knowledge, expertise, and leadership in the Salish language and culture into and among the people, in the present and future. The summertime camp approach is used in this project to add in learning experiences for children and youth. On a broad basis, language learning extends to the many tribal gatherings, ceremonies, and events each year, throughout the seasons (Real Bird, 2001, p. 2).

The Southern Ute Language Immersion School is located in Ignacio, Colorado. The school serves children from infancy to third grade. It is a Ute language immersion school, and utilizes the Anna Montessori teaching/learning methods. School director Carol Baker-Olguin describes the decision to adopt the Montessori method and language immersion: "The decision to design the Montessori school to serve children from infancy was to facilitate the language/culture component and eventually revival of the Ute language." Olguin is a professional Montessori teacher, and was instrumental in convincing the community of the merits of the Montessori methods. According to Olguin, the Ute community advisors thought the Montessori method "meshed well with the Native American thought and philosophy regarding teaching and learning methods. The self-paced learning and exploratory aspects were especially appealing."

The Southern Ute School is private, supported by the tribal council through casino-earned appropriations. They have chosen not to seek federal funding, private sector or state funds. Olguin explains, "The decision was based on the tribe's desire to serve only Southern Ute tribal members or direct descendants of tribal members. The tribe did not want to be encumbered by federal regulations." Moreover, the tribe designed a five-year plan, and made a commitment to school support. The school advisors have discussed the need for an endowment to be developed "to continue the operations of the school unencumbered by tribal politics." Olguin noted that the school future is at the whim of the tribal council, and council priorities may change from year to year; "the commitment (to the school) is dependent on the politics of the council and its leadership." The tribal council commitment entailed the building of a school facility, as well as the school's operational funds ((C. Baker-Olguin, interview, August 18, 2001).

The five-year plan encompasses training Montessori/Ute language teachers, as well. The school partners with a nearby university for the Montessori teacher certification. The university mentors provide methods training, and this combines with the Ute language fluency of the teacher trainees. The school director described the Montessori courses required of the trainees as "rigorous." The teacher training coursework compounds with the weight of daily teaching responsibility with the children. During the initial year, 18 tribal members began the training, and five completed. The rigors of this training and teaching proved to be daunting. Carol Olguin attributed trainee attrition to the lack of academic preparation, a limited number of Ute speakers, and too few applicants for the project trainee positions. The school's greatest challenge is finding potential teachers among a small number of Ute speakers. The school director stated, "This is seen as a major problem at present in obtaining the goal of language revival in an immersion setting."

Conclusions

Native American language immersion is a recent phenomenon in Indigenous, Native, and tribal communities in the United States. Fifty Native American groups are currently engaged in language immersion planning and operation. These Native language teaching and learning efforts include year-round schools, summer and seasonal camps, and weekend retreats and seminars. The schools, camps, and programs rely exclusively on the tribal language as the teaching and learning medium.

The Navajo community school of Rough Rock, Arizona, has successfully provided their children language immersion for over 20 years. Native family groups and elders have organized Native American language immersion schools among the Blackfeet, Ojibway, and the Assiniboine/Sioux people. Summer and seasonal camps and training seminars have built language understanding for participants of all ages for Northern Cheyenne, Ojibway, and Crow children. Language immersion preschools currently serve several hundred children from the Ojibway, Cree, Assiniboine, and Ute nations. Tribal language commissions and cultural authorities have mandated cultural and language learning, that includes leadership training, language teaching, and certification. Master/apprenticeship relationships have developed for culture and language learning among the Salish Kootenai of Montana, the Northern Cheyenne of Montana, and the Three Affiliated Tribes of North Dakota—the Mandan, Hidatsa, and Arikara. For Indigenous people, these Native American language immersion activities hold great promise in the development of children, youth, family, and community.

Native language educators and activists have taken up the difficult and urgent work of Native language preservation with devotion and commitment. First, there are those who recognize the serious rate of language loss and have made a lifetime commitment to tribal language restoration, for the vitality of the tribal nation and its future. Second, Native American children and youth have exhibited stagnant educational achievement (among the poorest achievement of all American ethnic groups). Native language immersion has demonstrated remarkable promise in participants' educational achievement. A third source of motivation to Native language immersion is the greater cultural and language preservation or revitalization effort that strengthens and rebuilds the Native community. Fourth, culture and language teaching and participation positively correlate with Native student retention rates. Fifth, Native leaders foresee a world in urgent need of Native perspectives or worldview in areas including childrearing, natural resources management, and family and community development. Finally, there are a few activists who are motivated to this work by its political potential to allay the centuries-old history of injury and subjugation of Native people. This study has analyzed these factors, and delineated, from the voices of Native language immersion teachers, parents, and students, the attributes of Native American and Indigenous language immersion schools, camps and projects.

Native language immersion is a practice or methodology of language learning that concentrates on communication, exclusively in the Native language. Total physical response, TPR, is the primary methodology for the Native language immersion classrooms, camps, and projects. Virtually all of the Native language immersion activities are carried out in the context of the tribal or Indigenous culture. Many immersion schools are built and furnished after "gramma's home" and pattern their methods from Native grandparents' ways of knowing and learning. The teachers, educators, and activists have diverse backgrounds; by profession/vocation, they are teachers, bus drivers, retired BIA administrators, Head Start teachers, ranchers, and more. These educators and activists have a driving, even compelling commitment to language learning and a wellspring of enthusiasm for their students' and participants' potential for speaking and communicating in the tribal language. The students are toddlers and children, middle and high school students, young adults, parents of young children, adults, and elders. Where immersion is happening, all ages of Native people are pursuing the goal of speaking their Native language.

The tribal colleges and universities of this country play a leading role in Native language immersion. They are engaging their entire communities through college student development, community-based projects, school-aged educational services, and early childhood education opportunities. The language immersion approaches are experiential, and place tribal elders and scholars at the center of the language immersion activities. Children, youth, and college students hold a strategic place among the generations of Native people, and with language knowledge they are positively influential as siblings, parents of young children, children of elder parents, and grandparents. The tribal colleges recognize the language and culture as central to the education of the people for their health and wellbeing.

The Native language immersion activities have become a significant part of Native life in over 50 locations across the nation. For these communities, educators and activists have designed and implemented language learning experiences that are unprecedented in their positive impact on education, individual and family strengthening, intergenerational partnerships, and tribal health and wellbeing. As a relatively new educational phenomenon, it is not yet a movement. The educators and activists have developed unique and custom designed strategies to deliver Native language immersion. While activists collaborate locally and occasionally between projects, the commitment, creativity, expertise, courage, and fortitude that must be present in the schools and camps preclude a "get on the band wagon" potential. Native language immersion is difficult work; work fit only for those few whose devotion to the tribal language (for whatever reason) is unstoppable. This work requires knowing the tribal language and perseverance beyond all measure.

The support for language immersion is problematic. Language immersion costs money, money that most tribal groups can hardly spare in the face of demanding issues in education, health, housing, and natural resources management. Federal funds support language preservation, but are seriously insufficient, short term, and only incidentally supportive of language immersion. Public schools regulations and requirements pose difficult hurdles, although Native Hawaiian language immersion has acquired a place in the public school structure, both directly and through the charter school structure. The Diné and Ojibway people have set this example, through tribal and community-based initiatives and the new federal charter school structure. Private sector support has been instrumental in the development of language immersion; some language immersion schools accept private funding only. Native groups who seek private funding for language immersion face formidable challenges:

- Native American language immersion and its meaning to American Indian communities is relatively unknown to foundation decision makers. Native language immersion is making a difference in education, quality of life, student retention, and family and community strength. All these factors are meaningful.

- Native communities must have contacts with the private sector. Foundation program officers must somehow make effective connections with language immersion educators. This is a special challenge since many are tribal elders and traditionalists.

- Language immersion schools and camps need long-term and less categorical support. Language immersion education takes time to develop, perhaps five to seven years, just to get started. Broad guidelines that respect and appreciate the Native methods, and interdisciplinary nature of language immersion will be needed for a "fit" into the foundation programs. Native language immersion is education, culture, language, community, family, leadership, and children and youth programming.

- Native communities have urgent social, educational, and economic issues, and cannot rely on tribal resources. Matching fund requirements are difficult to make.

- Only 50 of the nation's 500 federally recognized tribes have profitable casino enterprises. Language immersion schools are unlikely to come from casino tribes. Misperceptions exist about casino wealth that causes trouble for fundraisers and American Indians, generally. Some Indian tribes are wealthy, but the grand majority are remarkably impoverished.

- American Indians are less than 1% of the American population, a proportionately small number. Still, 1.8 million American Indian people should not suffer invisibility. Studies do exist, data is available, and informed decision making is possible.

Native American language immersion schools, camps, and activities have benefited from the language resurgence and immersion models of the Native Hawaiians and the Maori of New Zealand. During the past two decades, both Hawaiian and Maori communities have created and implemented language immersion preschools, schools and colleges. Indigenous language immersion has made astounding records of educational achievement among the children, youth, and adult participants in language immersion education schools. Language immersion clearly has a critical role in educational Indigenous and Native American development.

Most intriguing about the Native and Indigenous language immersion models is the clear and positive connection between Native and Indigenous language and culture with educational achievement (Benham & Mann, 2003, p. 177). Native and tribal communities ascribe to this principle, through the language immersion schools, camps, and community/family based projects. Now, Native and Indigenous peoples can strengthen the practice and validate this language immersion model, for the essentiality of culture and language as a function of knowing and learning. Knowing and learning are recognized as the foundation of health and wellbeing for all human communities around the world. Native American language immersion is a source of hope for Native America; it is innovative education for Native children and families.

Janine Pease, EdD (Crow), served as president of Little Big Horn College, where she played a major role in the tribal languages collaborative among Montana tribal colleges, the Learning Lodge Institute.

References

Aha Punana, L. (n.d.). Our Language: E Ola Ka Olelo Hawaii—the Hawaiian Language Shall Live. Retrieved from http://www.ahapunanaleo.org/HTML/OL.htm

Benham, M.K.P., & Mann, H. (2003). Culture and Language Matters: Defining, Implementing, and Evaluating. In M.K.P. Benham & W.J. Stein (Eds.), *The Renaissance of American Indian Higher Education: Capturing the Dream* (pp. 167–192). London: Lawrence Erlbaum Associates.

Bielenberg, B. (1999). Indigenous Language Codification: Cultural Effects. In J. Reyhner, G. Cantoni, R.N. St. Clair, & E.P. Yazzie (Eds.), *Revitalizing Indigenous Languages* (pp. 103–112). Flagstaff: Northern Arizona University.

Boyer, P. (2000). Learning Lodge Institute: Montana Colleges Empower Cultures to Save Languages. *Tribal College: Journal of American Indian Higher Education, 11*(3), 12–14.

Burnaby, B. (1996). Aboriginal Language Maintenance, Development, and Enhancement: A Review of Literature. In G. Cantoni (Ed.), *Stabilizing Indigenous Languages*, pp. 22–40. Flagstaff: Center for Excellence in Education, Northern Arizona University.

Cantoni, G.B. (1999). Using TPR—Storytelling to Develop Fluency and Literacy in Native American Languages. In J. Reyhner, G. Cantoni, R.N. St. Clair, & E.P. Yazzie (Eds.), *Revitalizing Indigenous Languages* (pp. 53–58). Flagstaff: Northern Arizona University.

Crawford, J. (1994). Endangered Native American Languages: What Is to Be Done, and Why? Washington, DC: National Clearinghouse on Bilingual Education.

Dale, J. (2000). Rekindling the Anishnabe Language Fires at Bay Mills. *Tribal College: Journal of American Indian Higher Education, 11*(3), 22–23.

Demmert, W. (1994). Blueprints for Indian Education: Languages and Cultures. *ERIC Digest*, ED372899, 1–7.

Demmert, W., & Arnold, R. (1996). Language Policy. In *Stabilizing Indigenous Languages*. Flagstaff: Center for Excellence in Education, Northern Arizona University.

Gipp, G.E. (2003). Foreword. In M.K.P. Benham & W.J. Stein (Eds.), *The Renaissance of American Indian Higher Education: Capturing the Dream* (pp. xiii–xvi). London: Lawrence Erlbaum Associates.

Hadderman, M. (1998). Charter Schools. *ERIC Digest*, ED422600, 1–3.

Hakuta, K. (2001, April 13). Testimony to the United States Commission on Civil Rights. The Education of Language Minority Students.

Howard, E.R., & Loeb, M.I. (1998). In Their Own Words: Two-Way Immersion Teachers Talk about Their Professional Experiences. *ERIC Digest*, EDO-FL-98014, 1–4.

Howard, E.R., & Sugarman, J. (2001). Two-Way Immersion Programs: Features and Statistics. *ERIC Digest*, EDO-FL-01-01, 1–2.

Iñupiaq Immersion School. (2001, October). A Presentation on Iñupiaq Immersion School at the National Indian Education Association Conference, Billings, Montana.

Keami, S. (2000). Advocating for a Stimulating and Language-Based Education. In M.K.P. Benham & W.J. Stein (Eds.), *Indigenous Educational Models for Contemporary Practice: In Our Mother's Voice* (pp. 51–59). London: Lawrence Erlbaum Associates.

Kipp, D.R. (2000). Commitment to Language-Based Education. In M.K.P. Benham & W.J. Stein (Eds.), *Indigenous Educational Models for Contemporary Practice: In Our Mother's Voice* (pp. 62–69). London: Lawrence Erlbaum Associates.

Kipp, D.R. (2000). *Encouragement, Guidance, Insights and Lessons for Native Language Activists Developing Their Own language Programs*. Saint Paul, MN: Piegan Institute with the Grotto Foundation.

LaFortune, R. (2000). *Native Languages as World Languages: A Vision for Assessing and Sharing Information about Native Languages across Grant-Making Sectors*. Saint Paul, MN: Grotto Foundation.

Littlebear, R. (1999). To Save Our Languages, We Must Change Our Teaching Methods. *Tribal College: Journal of American Indian Higher Education, 11*(3), 18–20.

Marcos, K. (2001). *Why, How, and When Should My Child Learn a Second Language*. Rockville, MD: ERIC Educational Resources Center.

McCarty, T.L., & Dick, G.S. (2000). Mother Tongue Literacy and Language Renewal: The Case of the Navajo. *Proceedings of the 1996 World Conference on Literacy*. Tucson: University of Arizona.

Mistaken Chief, D., Sr. (1999). Using Blackfoot Language to Rediscover Who We Are. *Tribal College: Journal of American Indian Higher Education, 11*(3), 26–28.

Nijhuis, M. (2002, June 11). Tribal Immersion Schools Rescue Language and Culture. *The Christian Science Monitor.*

Parks, D.R., Kushner, J., Hooper, W., & Flavin, F. (1999). Documenting and Maintaining Native American Language in the 21st Century: The Indiana University Model. In J. Reyhner, G. Cantoni, R.N. St. Clair, & E.P. Yazzie (Eds.), *Revitalizing Indigenous Languages* (pp. 59–83). Flagstaff: Northern Arizona University.

Peacock, T.D., & Day, D.R. (1999). Teaching American Indian and Alaska Native Languages in the Schools: What Has Been Learned. *ERIC Digest,* ED438155, 1–8.

Pease-Pretty On Top, J. (2000). *Native Ways of Knowing and Learning.* Paper presented at the Crow Education Summit of 2001, Crow Agency, MT.

Pease-Pretty On Top, J. (2002). Bringing Thunder. *Tribal College: Journal of American Indian Higher Education, 14*(1), 10–13.

Real Bird, L. (2000). Empowering and Redefining the Languages. *Ash-ammaa-ehkuua: Newsletter of the Learning Lodge Institute, 1*(1).

Real Bird, L. (2000). Formalization of Native Languages and Cultures through Teaching and Learning. *Ash-ammaa-ehkuua: Newsletter of the Learning Lodge Institute, 1*(1).

Rubin, D.S. (1999). Sm'algyax Language Renewal: Prospects and Options. In J. Reyhner, G. Cantoni, R.N. St. Clair, & E.P. Yazzie (Eds.), *Revitalizing Indigenous Languages* (pp. 17–32). Flagstaff: Northern Arizona University.

Selden, R. (2000, June 28). Immersion Programs Ensure Cultural Survival. *Indian Country Today,* pp. 1–3.

Silva, K. (2000). Revitalizing Culture and Language: Returning to the Land. In M.K.P. Benham & W.J. Stein (Eds), *Indigenous Educational Models for Contemporary Practice: In Our Mother's Voice* (pp. 71–79). London: Lawrence Erlbaum Associates.

Stein, W.J. (2003). Developmental Action for an Indigenous College. In M.K.P. Benham & W.J. Stein (Eds.), *The Renaissance of American Indian Higher Education: Capturing the Dream* (pp. 25–60). London: Lawrence Erlbaum Associates.

Sugarman, J., & Howard, L. (2001). Two-Way Immersion Shows Promising Results: Findings from a New Study. *ERIC/CLL Language Link, ERIC Clearinghouse on Languages and Linguistics.*

Tribal College: Journal of American Indian Higher Education. (2000). Little Priest Immerses Students in Language. *Tribal College: Journal of American Indian Higher Education, 11*(3), 28.

www.ingramcontent.com/pod-product-compliance
Lightning Source LLC
Chambersburg PA
CBHW020108020526
44112CB00033B/1093